PSYCHOLOGY LIBRARY EDITIONS:
HISTORY OF PSYCHOLOGY

Volume 8

AN INQUIRY INTO THE FOUNDATIONS OF PSYCHOLOGY

AN INQUIRY INTO THE FOUNDATIONS OF PSYCHOLOGY

PER SAUGSTAD

Routledge
Taylor & Francis Group

LONDON AND NEW YORK

First published in Great Britain 1965 by George Allen & Unwin Ltd

This edition first published in 2020
by Routledge
2 Park Square, Milton Park, Abingdon, Oxon OX14 4RN

and by Routledge
52 Vanderbilt Avenue, New York, NY 10017

Routledge is an imprint of the Taylor & Francis Group, an informa business

British Library Cataloguing in Publication Data
A catalogue record for this book is available from the British Library

ISBN: 978-0-367-40845-9 (Set)
ISBN: 978-1-00-301614-4 (Set) (ebk)
ISBN: 978-0-367-85711-0 (Volume 8) (hbk)
ISBN: 978-0-367-85721-9 (Volume 8) (pbk)
ISBN: 978-1-00-301454-6 (Volume 8) (ebk)

Publisher's Note
The publisher has gone to great lengths to ensure the quality of this reprint but points out that some imperfections in the original copies may be apparent.

Disclaimer
The publisher has made every effort to trace copyright holders and would welcome correspondence from those they have been unable to trace.

An Inquiry into the Foundations of Psychology

BY

PER SAUGSTAD

OSLO

UNIVERSITETSFORLAGET

LONDON

ALLEN & UNWIN

NEW YORK

THE BEDMINSTER PRESS

Published simultaneously in

the United States of America by
THE BEDMINSTER PRESS, INCORPORATED,
Vreeland Avenue, Totowa, 07512, New Jersey.
Library of Congress Catalogue Card Number 65-28894.

in the British Commonwealth by
GEORGE ALLEN & UNWIN LTD, LONDON,

and in Scandinavia for Scandinavian University Books by
UNIVERSITETSFORLAGET, OSLO

AAS & WAHLS BOKTRYKKERI, OSLO

To Professor Edgar Tranekjær Rasmussen
and
the late Professor Edward C. Tolman

Contents

Preface

Psychology is in a period of explosive expansion. New problem areas are incessantly being opened, a variety of new techniques introduced, and countless theories advanced. In this period of expansion I have made a halt in an effort to clarify basic assumptions on which modern psychology rests. My inquiry originated in an attempt to evaluate my own research in the area of thinking. Here certain problems obtruded themselves. In what sense was my work experimental? What was the relationship of thought processes to perceptual processes, and how were both types of processes affected by learning? There was also the problem of circularity of reasoning, which tended to emerge each time I was making a theoretical statement. Also, the problem of the reproducibility of the experimental results was repeatedly encountered as a result of failures to duplicate well-known experiments.

This attempt to clarify the problems raised by my own research work led to an examination of related areas in modern as well as earlier periods of experimental psychology. This examination revealed that the same problems were inherent in psychological research work of all periods. This has convinced me that psychology is ripe for a Machian purge. As long as psychologists are dominated by an impatient desire to expand their area of research, progress will be slow. The same mistakes will be repeated and basic assumptions remain unanalysed. The introduction of methodological principles from philosophy or from other branches of science can only lead to a superficial treatment of psychological problems. A fruitful methodology for psychological research can be developed solely by a patient analysis of basic assumptions.

I have dedicated this book to my two teachers and friends, Professor Edgar Tranekjær Rasmussen, University of Copenhagen, and the late Professor Edward C. Tolman, University of California. In admiration and respect for both I have struggled to reconcile the behavioristic position of Tolman to the phenomenological orientation of Tranekjær Rasmussen. In this struggle Professor Kai von Fieandt, University of Helsinki, has given me invaluable assistance. On innumerable occasions I have profited from his great knowledge of perception and his balanced points of view.

I am indebted to my colleagues of some years' standing, Ivar Lie and Arild Lian, for helping to guide my thinking out of the blind alleys into which it has had a marked tendency to enter. I am grateful to them for their stimulating criticism. My assistant Lars Smith has also helped to clarify knotty problems of which there certainly is an abundance. Kenneth Junge has advised me in problems of psychophysics.

On a number of occasions I had given up completing this inquiry, despairing over the intricacy of the problems. That I have carried it through is due to my wife Letten. She has discussed all points with me, the major as well as the minor ones.

Oslo, December, 1964

Per Saugstad

Introduction

This is a book about observations in scientific psychology. The point of view to be presented is that isolated sets of observations cannot serve as the basis for a scientific system or a theory in psychology. A scientific psychology requires that the relationship between a number of sets of different observations be specified by rigorous definitions independent of theory. If this point of view is accepted our conception of what constitutes a scientific psychology will be radically changed.

The problem of observations in psychology was forced upon me in an attempt to clarify the term 'perception'. In a study of the treatment of problems of perception in the history of psychology from Fechner and Helmholtz to the present, I found that theorists again and again confused observation and theoretical statement. This confusion was evident in all periods in the history of psychology.

First, it was encountered in the treatment of the term 'stimulus' by Hull (1943) and other leading behavioristic psychologists. The research worker familiar with the study of perception will at once notice that the term 'stimulus' is left undefined in Hull and other stimulus-response theorists. These theorists proceed on the assumption that when some type of behavior, some response, has been registered, there must also exist some stimulus. The term 'stimulus' is just inferred from the registration of some type of behavior. There is nothing erroneous about this assumption, but what is not realized is that before the stimulus as well as the response have been determined no scientific problem of psychology can be formulated. The research worker, having merely registered a certain type of behavior, and thus being in the possession of merely a set of responses, will necessarily have to use his observations as theoretical constructs, as concepts. As a result it cannot be decided whether the reasoning is circular, empty of empirical meaning.

Secondly I encountered the confusion of theoretical statement and observation in the Gestalt laws of perceptual organization as originally formulated by Wertheimer (1923). The first two of these so-called laws, the two most clearly stated, apparently are empty of empirical meaning. The tendency to make what may be empirically empty statements also seems to inhere in Rubin's (1915) approach to the study of the problem of figure-ground. On the whole, there seems to be a widespread tendency in phenomenology to confuse theoretical construct and observation.

Thirdly, Garner, Hake, and Eriksen (1956) called my attention to the unoperational procedure of Stevens (1960) and other research workers using the so-called direct scaling technique in psychophysics. In examining the procedure in question I was convinced that the point made by Garner, Hake, and Eriksen is correct. Clearly, the research workers in this approach to psychophysical scaling cannot state what is scaled by their procedure. In order to clarify the problems involved in the direct scaling technique the methodological position of modern research workers like Stevens and Graham (1951, 1958) was compared to that of the pioneer psychophysicists. It was found that the former tended to leave the reference to conscious experience involved in all psychophysical research unconsidered. When this reference is omitted, studies in psychophysics easily become empirically meaningless. In the psychophysical formula $R = f(S)$, where S denotes some physical dimension and R a set of responses, R cannot be specified operationally, unless the instructions are included in the operational definitions. If the instructions given in the psychophysical experiment are not included in the analysis of the experiment, no logical inference is possible. The instructions cannot be treated as belonging under the systematic, the independent variables, nor as belonging under the dependent variables. The instructions form part of the theoretical construct involved. Actually the position of modern research workers, like that of Stevens and Graham, leads to an inability to distinguish between the independent and dependent experi-

12

mental variables. This was exactly what was found to be involved in the statements of Hull and Wertheimer.

The examination of the treatment of perceptual problems in psychology thus revealed that in behavioristics, phenomenology, as well as in psychophysics, old and new, there was a pronounced tendency to produce empirically empty statements. Common to all periods in the study of psychology is a lack of empirically established concepts. In all periods the observations tend to serve the double role of observation and theoretical construct. It looked as if psychologists invariably provided their observations with some speculative element.

As a result of the repeated encounter in psychological literature with a confusion of theoretical statement and observation, the question raised itself: is the task of the psychologist of such a nature that this confusion necessarily arises? The answer that finally presented itself was: by necessity the attempt to relate by some theoretical statement what may be referred to as isolated sets of observations, is bound to result in the addition of some speculative element which will contaminate the observations. Since this answer to the question may radically change our conception of what constitutes a scientific psychology, I will first examine previous conceptions of a scientific psychology. Then I shall present an alternative to these conceptions.

History of psychology in outline

A characteristic of psychology as a science appears to be that it has been founded a number of times. The first founding is usually attributed to Wundt, who declared that psychology should be a science and proceeded to establish the first laboratory in 1879. For about three decades both content and methods of the new psychology were to a large extent determined by conceptions current in Wundt's laboratory. A second founding may be said to have occurred when the phenomenological orientation became dominant in the study of perception about 1910. In the U.S.A. the phenomenological approach gained recognition mainly thorugh the Berlin Gestaltists, Wertheimer, Köhler, and Koffka. A better perspective on the history is probably achieved if not only the Berlin Gestaltists, but the phenomenological movement from the beginning of this century is included. Then, attention is given to the man who was probably the chief inspirer, Husserl, and also to research workers like Katz and Rubin, who were outside the group of Berlin Gestaltists. If Husserl is included, the continuity in the phenomenological movement from the early part of the century to the modern era is established.

The third founding to which we will refer is that of behavioristic psychologists in the 1930s. One may date behaviorism to the time when the phenomenological movement took possession of the psychology of perception. However, since behaviorism in the 1930s was modified in important respects under the influence of logical positivism, it may be more reasonable to date the third founding to the 1930s, and refer to the approach to psychology resulting as that of behavioristics.

There is, of course, some continuity in the history of psychology, but the changes taking place in the orientation of the leading psychologists at the moments indicated are so drastic that it is warranted to speak of three different periods. In each period there is a rejection of the work and thinking of the previous period. The research workers in each period are impatiently pushing forward to realize their programs for a scientific psychology. The rejection of the previous thinking is probably most pronounced in behavioristics. There is not much left of the older psychology in Watson (1929), Guthrie (1935), Hull (1943), Spence (1951), Skinner (1938), and even in Tolman (1932), who was more concerned with earlier positions taken. In retrospect it seems fair to state that theory construction in the stimulus-response approach probably would have proceeded along different lines if the research workers had engaged in a patient study of the problems ot perception. Further I believe that a careful consideration of Mach might have purged behavioristic psychology of its tendency to conceive of the act, or of behavior, in some mystic fashion.

There is also an uncompromising rejection of earlier psychology by the phenomenologists. Obviously the phenomenologists would have learnt a lot from the thinking of great experimentalists like Helmholtz, Fechner, and Ebbinghaus, and again Mach might also have rescued them from extreme points of view. As a matter of fact, the phenomenologists probably took over more of the older psychology than admitted. Thus Katz (1930) was not only more influenced by Hering (1905—20) than he expressed in his book on color, but he was also profoundly influenced by Helmholtz (1856 —66). Wertheimer (1923), in the formulation of his Gestalt laws, may have been strongly influenced by Mach's (1886) treatment of the problems of form perception.

In each period of psychology the research workers claimed to have new methods and new theoretical constructs. However, what seems clear is that each time psychology was founded there was no clear conception of what psychology was about. The Wundtian introspectionists, the phenomenologists, and the behavioristic psychologists were all equally vague about the task confronting the psychologist. None of them were able to specify what could be meant by a problem in a scientific psychology. Still they were all convinced that they

15

conceived of psychology in a manner different from their precursors. Obviously, the phenomenological research workers on perception were interested in other problems than the earlier workers in psychophysics, but did they possess different methods? In the same way behavioristic psychologists were interested in other problems than both the introspectionists and the phenomenologists, but again did they possess different methods? Apparently, as long as none of them was able to specify what constitutes the task of the psychologist, we are in no position to answer these questions. Let us examine the different declarations concerning the task of the psychologist a little more carefully.

Wundt (1874) and his students claimed to have a new method, that of introspection, to avail themselves of the experiment, and to be in possession of a key term to psychological theorizing, that of the sensation. The introspective method was used in conjunction with the experiment. In early psychology conceptions about the method of introspection were intimately connected with conceptions of the sensation. In the psychology of Wundt (1874) and Titchner (1896) the sensation is neither regarded as something to be directly observed, nor as a theoretical construct, or a concept, to be empirically determined. It is conceived of as an invariable element of consciousness. This explains why the method of introspection is stated in such an indeterminate manner. Thus Titchner (1896, p. 33) wrote:

The rule for introspection, in the sphere of sensation, is as follows: *Be as attentive as possible to the object or process which gives rise to the sensation, and, when the object is removed or the process completed, recall the sensation by an act of memory as vividly and completely as you can.*

It is not possible to decide whether the sensation is to be established as a theoretical construct or whether it is something to be directly observed. As is easily seen, essential points have not received specification. Thus we do not know in what our being attentive should consist, nor what an object or process is, nor when the process may be regarded as completed, nor what can be meant by an act of memory, etc. An examination of the early works of psychology (Wundt, 1874; Titchner, 1896; Ebbinghaus, 1902; Stumpf, 1906) reveals no clearer conception of the task of the psychologist.

Early introspective psychology may be characterized as a quest for invariable elements on which to base a scientific psychology. Thus Titchner (1896, p. 28) wrote about the sensation:

Whatever test we put it to, — however persistent our attempt at analysis and however refined our method of investigation, — we end where we began: The sensation remains precisely what it was before we attacked it.

A tendency to conceive of the sensations as invariable elements is also noticeable in the great research workers on the study of perception, in Helmholtz (1856—66), Fechner (1860) and Mach (1886). Sensations are regarded as the events on which not only physics, but also psychology is to rest. The fact that physics rests on observational reports of experiences subsumed under the term 'sensation' did of course strengthen the belief among psychologists that the sensation was some fundamental element in consciousness, something endowed with an *a priori* objectivity. However, it should not be overlooked that the early psychophysicists frequently established their sensations as experimentally defined concepts, but they were not always able to handle their concepts in a consistent manner. In the chapter on psychophysics we shall see that the conception of the sensation as an invariable element in consciousness has been reintroduced to modern psychology by Stevens (1960) and his followers in their development of the so-called direct scaling technique.

The quest for the invariable element, for the objective event, on which to base a scientific psychology is actually a characteristic of psychological thinking in all three periods. The phenomenologists objected to the belief in the sensations as invariable elements in consciousness. They pointed out that sensations were always experienced as parts of wholes and that their character depended upon the whole or structure of

2

which they formed part. The wholes, Gestalts, or thing-likenesses were not further analyzable. However, as in the previous period there was a tendency to endow the constructs with an *a priori* objectivity and to conceive of wholes or Gestalts as something neither directly observable nor definable by reference to observations.

The phenomenologists rejected the method of introspection. Instead they offered the phenomenological description. It was as a result of this method that the wholes, Gestalts or thinglikenesses emerged. Unfortunately, as happened in the previous period, none of the thinkers or research workers in the phenomenological movement were able explicitly to state their method. In the phenomenological writing there is an abundance of interesting points of view, but one searches in vain for an explanation of what constitutes the phenomenological method (cf. Husserl, 1913; Katz, 1930; Koffka, 1935; Köhler, 1938; McLeod, 1951; Merleau-Ponty, 1945; Rubin, 1915, 1927; Tranekjær Rasmussen, 1956; Wertheimer, 1923). The writers restrict themselves to emphasizing that the research worker, in describing his experiences, must assume a naive, unreflective, unsophisticated attitude, that he must not confuse his immediate experiences with his knowledge about objects and events.

Behavioristic psychologists objected to the conception of the human subject as the observer in introspective and phenomenological studies. If the person serving as the subject is regarded as an observer, he is clearly invested with a double role. The events on which he is to report, such as experiences of hues, pitches, or of thoughts, form part of the theoretical constructs. Thus the subject will necessarily have to decide on theoretical issues in giving his report. Conceiving of the subject as an observer would erase the distinction between observed event and theoretical statement. Therefore, the behavioristic psychologist claimed that the person serving as the subject must not be regarded as an observer. The observer in the experiment is the experimenter registering the responses of the subject. Theoretical statements should be based on these responses. Clearly, this requirement must be accepted if rigorous definitions are to be possible. The behavioristic position

18

with regard to the person serving as the subject in psychological studies is summed up by Spence (1948) in the following way:

In other words, the events studied by the psychologist, Watson held, should consist in observations of the overt behavior of *other* organisms, other persons than the observing scientist himself, and not in the observation of the scientist's own internal activities.

The insistence that the theoretical statements have to be based on the responses emitted by the organism studied is probably the main contribution of behavioristics towards a conception of what constitutes a scientific psychology.

However, in insisting that the human subject in psychological studies ought not to play the double role of observer and theorist, behavioristic psychologists have failed to examine the problem of ascertaining whether or not the theorist endows the events contained in the observations with meaning, thus confusing observed event and theoretical statement. Behavioristic psychologists, in their firm belief that behavior is objective, do not even seem to have raised this problem. If the responses observed could be treated as the events subjected to a study in natural science, the problem would hardly be an obtrusive one. Obviously responses cannot be treated in this way.

The responses omitted belong to a perceiving and thinking organism. Thinking here refers to the fact that the organism studied is able to capitalize on stimulation received at points in time prior to the period in which it is studied. It is difficult to realize how the psychologist can possibly be in a position to make rigorous statements about the responses emitted before he has gained a scientific knowledge of the perceptual and thought processes in the organism. Analyses of the theoretical formulations of leading behavioristic thinkers such as Hull (1943), Spence (1951), Guthrie (1959), Skinner (1938, 1959), Estes (1959) reveal that these processes are not subjected to a scientific study. In a recent behavioristic evaluation of psychology as a science (Koch, 1959) the study of thinking is not even included in the treatment of the basic psychological processes. The belief of the behavioristic psychologist that a consideration of perceptual and thought processes may be avoided in the study of behavior, arouses the suspicion that at some point behavioristic psychology must be based on an untenable assumption.

Apparently perceptual and thought processes must enter into psychological theorizing at some point. The behavioristic psychologist introduces these processes indirectly when he is relating his responses to other types of responses. The question, therefore, arises: Is this introduction of perceptual and thought processes in accordance with the basic rules of science? The answer must be no.

To make clear that the behavioristic psychologist resorts to his perceptual and thought experiences in a way incompatible with the rules of science, we shall begin by examining the term behaviour. Watson (1929) made the following statement about the new psychology:

For the behaviorist, psychology is that division of natural science which takes human behavior — the doings and sayings, both learned and unlearned, of people as its subject matter. It is the study of what people do from even before birth until death.

This statement reveals a basic confusion in Watson's conception of psychology. Is behavior to be regarded as the events to be reported upon in the observations or is it to be regarded as processes in the organism studied? Obviously, to live up to his criticism of the introspective and phenomenological psychology, the behavioristic psychologist must regard behavior as the events to be reported upon in the observations. This means that the only assumption he can make about these events is their existence. Behavior cannot, as an observed event, be endowed with meaning. But if behavior cannot be endowed with meaning, it cannot be related to the organism studied. Thus the behavioristic psychology lacks a reference to the organism being studied.

This fundamental point never seems to have been realized by behavioristic psychologists. Apparently they have confused behavior as an event in their immediate consciousness with an event in another organism. It is solely in the latter sense that behavior can be regarded as an objective event. I shall expand upon this point in the chapter on behavioristics. Here I shall merely call attention to the fact that an operational specification of a set of responses can only provide us with events in terms of our immediate consciousness.

The behavioristic psychologist after merely specifying operationally a number of sets of responses is in no position to relate these sets to each other in a rigorous way. Rigorous scientific reasoning requires that solely the existence of these responses is assumed. If the research worker relates different sets of responses to each other, he obviously has to resort to his own perceptual and thought processes. These processes are unknown to him. Since these processes are unknown to him, he is in no position to ascertain that he has not endowed the events reported upon in the observations with meaning. In other words he cannot distinguish between the events observed and his theoretical statements. For this reason what are at present designated as theories of behavior must necessarily lack the rigor of scientific systems. No application of principles from mathematics, statistics, physics, physiology, or philosophy of science can alter this state of affairs.

In this book an attempt will be made to demonstrate how the contents of consciousness, referred to as conscious elements, or experiences, may be treated in a way satisfying the rigor of science. It will be shown that the suggested way of formulating the problem of psychology will also give the definition of an event in another organism. This definition is clearly what the behavioristic psychologist has been aiming at, but which he could not achieve because he refused to conceive of the study of psychology as the study of consciousness. However, the formulation presented will rest on the requirement stated by the behavioristic psychologist that the theoretical statements have to be based on a set of antecedent conditions, such as the stimulation of the organism by some type of physical energy or the time interval during which the organism has been deprived of food, and some type of reaction describable in terms of specified movements or locomotions in the organism.

21

Toward a definition of psychology

In the last chapter the history of psychology was characterized as a quest for objective events on which to base a scientific system. Under the joint influences of behaviorism and logical positivism this quest culminated in the conception of objectivity determined as intersubjective agreement. According to this conception, an event is established as objective when agreement is obtained between the observational reports of a specified number of observers. Thus, by specifying the conditions under which the observational reports are to be made as well as the characteristics of a number of observers, the degree of objectivity of some event was held to be determined. Objectivity is, according to this conception, introduced by a convention, and can be determined empirically. A satisfactory degree of intersubjective agreement ascertains that the observations can be shared by other research workers and thus can form the basis for an adequate communication.

Actually the notion that a number of observers should agree in their observations can hardly be said to represent anything essentially new. The ideal of a scientific procedure has for hundreds of years been to obtain observational reports from different observers which show as high as possible a degree of intersubjective agreement. The rule of intersubjective agreement between different observers has for a long time been and still must be considered an indispensable one in science. It must also be admitted that the observations reported in earlier periods of psychology must frequently be rejected because they do not reach a sufficient degree of intersubjective agreement.

By the rule of intersubjective agreement we may ascertain what we may refer to as the occurrence, or existence, of the events on which the observational reports are based. By this rule we may acquire sets of observations, or reference points, for the psychological system we want to construct. However, we have not established an order, or a relationship, among our reference points. Objectivity in psychology requires that this order among the reference points, the observations, must be established by rigorous definitions. When this has been done theory construction can take place. All through the history of psychology it has been assumed that this order is to be established by theoretical statements. What is lacking in psychology are definitions of the events to be studied. It is in the difficulty of knowing what is being studied that the task of the psychologist differs from that of the research workers in the natural sciences. Obviously the task of accounting for the movements of a rat — not to speak of a human being — equipped with mechanisms for perception and thinking must be vastly more difficult than that of accounting for the movements of Galileo's rolling balls and swinging pendulums. In some way the difference between these two types of tasks has not been realized in psychology.

I shall begin by considering psychology as the study of consciousness and by discussing the requirements of an introspective and phenomenological psychology. Then I shall proceed to discuss the behavioristic conception of psychology. It will be shown that the requirements of a scientific psychology will be the same whether the approach is made in terms of conscious elements, experiences, or in terms of behavior. In conceiving of psychology as the study of conciousness research workers have taken their point of departure in experiences, such as hues, brightnesses, pitches, loudnesses, smells, tastes, directions, movements, velocities, sizes, shapes, appearances of whiteness, of pronouncedness of colors, appearances of figure-ground, of thing-likeness, of unities, or wholes, of groups, of objects, of words, of numbers, etc. The development of psychophysics proves that a rigorous system may be created by making this a point of departure. However, the requirements of such a system do not appear to have been discussed in a systematic manner.

In order to construct a rigorous empirical system it is essential that a clear distinction can be made between the events reported upon in the observations and the theoretical constructs, or concepts, of the system. If it is to be possible to carry out a rigorous argument, reference must ultimately be made to some events about which the only assumption is that they exist. These events cannot be defined and thus cannot have any meaning. They are reported upon in the observations, and the conditions under which they occur are specified. By the rule of intersubjective agreement their occurrence or existence is determined. These events will be referred to as the primitives of the system. In contrast to the primitives, the concepts derive their meaning by definition. In this definition reference is made to the primitives. If the distinction between the primitives and the concepts is wiped out, confusion will necessarily arise.

In the history of psychology the problem of distinguishing between the primitives of the system and the concepts has proved to be very intricate.

Apparently a fundamental problem in the study of consciousness stems from the fact that our thought processes are unknown to us. Our perceptual and cognitive world appears as ordered. The conscious elements are related to each other in innumerable ways. These relationships have been elaborated in different cultures and are describable in every-day language. Further, the various branches of science have developed new orders. However, the processes underlying the relationships of our perceptual and cognitive world as well as the processes underlying the orders developed in the various branches of science are unknown to us. Therefore, if we attempt to establish the relationship between the primitives of our system by resorting to our unknown thought processes, or to what Mach (1886) referred to as unanalyzed consciousness, we are unable to ascertain that we have not added meaning to our primitives. In other words we will wipe out the distinction between the events observed and the theoretical statements.

As mentioned in the introductory chapter, the problem of establishing a relationship between primitives was forced upon me as a result of a repeated encounter with what appeared to be circular or empty statements by leading psychological research workers of behavioristic as well as phenomenological and introspective orientation. After years of research on the thought processes it was natural for me to begin my inquiry by examining the role attributed to the thought processes in the making of theoretical statements in psychology. This inquiry resulted in the above statement that the relationship between primitives in a psychological system cannot be established by recourse to unknown thought processes. As will be understood, this problem, arising from the fact that our thought processes are unknown to us, does not merely represent a problem for the psychologist interested in philosophical subtleties. The problem is basic to the establishment of any system in psychology. The reason why the problem has not been faced by modern behavioristically oriented research workers is not that the problem is solved by the behavioristic approach, but simply because behavioristic psychology, as indicated in the last chapter, rests on certain assumptions which apparently have never been systematically examined.

As an attempt at solving the problem of establishing a relationship between primitives without resorting to unknown thought processes, I will suggest the following. The psychologist may construct his system in such a way that he introduces one set of conscious elements, or experiences, by a definition which is based upon two different sets of primitives. The following diagram illustrates the procedure:

Figure 1.

In Figure 1, A and R are two different sets of primitives. E is a set of experiences which is defined by means of A and R. By this definition we have established a relationship between A and R without having resorted to unknown thought processes.

This definition will represent the first step in the construction of a system dealing with conscious elements. By successively defining sets of experiences we will have established the relationship between pairs of sets of primitives. The sets of experiences thus defined may then again be related to each other by new definitions (see Figure 2).

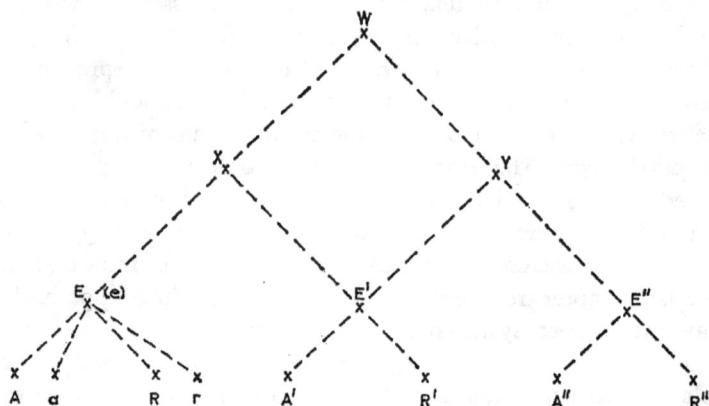

Figure 2.

In Figure 2, E, E' and E" represent different sets of experiences defined respectively by reference to A and R, A' and R', and to A" and R". X and Y are new sets of experiences defined by reference to E and E' and E' and E" respectively. Finally W is a set of experiences defined by reference to X and Y. We might also introduce a subset to one of the sets of experiences, for example e which is defined by reference to the two sets of primitives a and r.

By a series of successive definitions of the type indicated we might construct a system where every set of experiences introduced was rigorously defined in terms of one pair of primitives, or in terms of one pair of already defined sets of experiences. The system would of course be an arbitrary one, since its location in consciousness would not be known, but it would allow us to order conscious elements in a consistent manner. By means of the system we might order our perceptual and cognitive world in a way required by the rigor of scientific reasoning.

26

After having successfully established a number of definitions, we might proceed to develop theories to account for the relationships between the various sets of experiences defined.

In this abstract form I have presented the outline for a scientific system of psychology. Since the definitions would have to be established by experiment, the construction of such a system will require an enormous amount of creativity and will have to be worked out by generations of research workers. It must not be compared to speculative systems, such as those of Wundt (1874), and Hull (1943). This book is thus no presentation of such a system. It is the presentation of a conception of psychology. However, an approximation to the system suggested may be found in the psychophysics of color. The psychologist familiar with research on color vision (cf. Wright, 1946; Judd, 1951) may be able to concretize the conception advanced. By reference to Figure 2 we may state: E is a set of experiences of hue, A is a set of observations underlying the determination of the independent variable in terms of wavelength, R is a set of responses to changes in wavelength. The relationship between A and R is specified in terms of E, or E is defined in terms of A and R. The subset e is a set of experiences of hue where intensity of the light is varied, a being the set of observations underlying the determination of intensity of light, r the set of responses given to the changes in intensity. E' is a set of experiences of brightness, A' is a set of observations underlying the determination of the independent variable in terms of intensity, R' is a set of responses to changes in intensity. By means of E and E' we proceed to define luminosity (X). Actually we are not able to vary hue as an independent variable, nor to obtain a set of responses in terms of brightness. So we have to resort to the following design (see Figure 3):

We place two color patches (I and II) side by side and match the two patches for identity of experience of brightness. Then, we vary wavelength, specified by the set of observations A, and intensity, specified by the set of observations A'. Beforehand, we have defined E and E' in terms of A and R and A' and R' respectively. The design rests on the assumption of the identity of the experience of brightness of I and II.

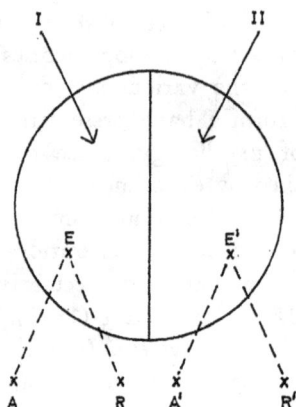

Figure 3.

It will be seen that we may continue by introducing new sets of experiences defined in the study of color. However, this may suffice to illustrate the diagram in Figure 2.

So far the task of the psychologist has been conceived of as that of defining one set of experiences by means of two sets of primitives. This definition must be established by experiment. This means that one of the sets of primitives must underlie a systematic, or independent variable, and one set a dependent variable. Actually, as was seen in the example of Figure 2 by the psychophysical study of color, the systematic, or independent variables rested on the concept of wavelength and on the concept of intensity of light respectively. Wavelength and intensity of light are constructions, and it is a complicated task to examine how these constructions are built up on primitives. However, this point is hardly of primary importance for the conception of psychology here advanced. The essential point to be made in this book is that a psychological concept must be based on a threefold reference. As long as it can be ascertained that the experiences underlying the systematic or independent variable are not identical to those to be defined, it hardly matters that the systematic variable rests on concepts of various types. However, instead of referring to a set of primitives underlying the systematic variable, I shall refer to a set of antecedent conditions, following here a widely accepted practice. The set of antecedent conditions may, as we have seen, be made up of conditions ascertaining, for example, a stimulation of some sensory organ with physical energy, or it may refer, for example, to conditions determining a certain amount of food deprivation.

We shall also select the primitives underlying the dependent variable, in accordance with a widely accepted practice, as some reaction in an organism, some movement of some part of the organism, or some locomotion of the organism as a whole. The reaction, referred to as the response, may thus be a signal by hand, a verbal statement, a turn of the organism to the right, etc. Usually the observational report will merely concern the occurrence or non-occurrence of the response. However, the response may also be describable in some quantitative fashion as an indication of strength of pressure by hand or number of drops of saliva. In both cases I shall refer to the primitives by the term set of responses. I shall designate this set of responses by the letter R. This term 'set of responses' refers only to the primitives underlying the dependent variable of one single experiment.

The conception of a set of antecedent conditions and a set of responses as the basis for a psychological system is a traditional one. However, what does not seem to have received proper emphasis is that in addition to a set of antecedent conditions and a set of responses, it is also necessary that a set of experiences is available. This set must be rigorously defined by means of the two other sets. What must be clear is that there is no scientific rule which may allow us to infer a relationship between a set of responses and a set of antecedent conditions underlying respectively a dependent variable and a systematic variable. This relationship can solely be established by a definition. It is by reference to a set of experiences that this relationship can be established. I shall return to this problem in the chapter on the experiment. Here the procedure for obtaining the definition will merely be illustrated by the definition of hue in psychophysics. We shall first assume, as was frequently the case in the pioneer work in psychophysics, that we perform the experiment on ourselves. So we serve both as subject and experimenter. In this experiment the set of antecedent conditions is made up of the conditions ascertaining a specified stimulation of the eye by light of different wavelengths. The set of reactions may consist in the marking of a sheet of paper in a specified manner. If the relationship between the set of responses, in this case indicated by the marks placed on the paper, and the set of antecedent conditions is a lawful one, and if it also can be demonstrated that this lawful relationship cannot be obtained in the way that we, as subjects, have availed ourselves of other experiences than those referred to as hue, we may proceed to define hue. The set of experiences called hue is then defined by reference to wavelength and a set of responses. We shall return to this definition later, in the chapter on psychophysics.

In the illustration of how hue was defined in psychophysics it was assumed that the experimenter also served as the subject. If we want to carry out the experiment on a person other than ourselves we will have to assume that this person is in the possession of the same experiences as we are. We have to make the inference from the set of antecedent conditions and the set of responses by an analogy to our own consciousness. Mach (1886) pointed out that we can only make a psychological study of another person by analogy to ourselves. However, this point was lost in behavioristics. Below we shall return to the behavioristic treatment of this fundamental problem.

The preceding discussion has led us to the conclusion that in order to be able to state a psychological problem we must be in the possession of: 1. a set of antecedent conditions, 2. a set of experiences, and 3. a set of responses. In order to avoid the wiping out of the distinction between the events observed and the theoretical statements the set of experiences must be rigorously defined by means of the set of antecedent conditions and the set of responses.

The conception of psychology advanced places the emphasis on the definition of the events to be studied. In this emphasis I seem to be in agreement with a conception of science indicated by Poincaré (1905). As will be known, Mach and Poincaré contributed greatly to the advancement of mechanics by emphasizing the need for rigorous definitions. In psychology the rigorous definition may be even more important in attempts at establishing a system, for the reason that the events to be studied here are far less distinguishable than those studied in physics when this science was developed.

If attempts are made to study consciousness without the establishment of rigorous definitions, the result will necessarily be that speculations have to be advanced about our consciousness more or less as a totality. By a rigorous definition we have determined what may be considered a reproducible event in our organism. It seems reasonable to believe that we have succeeded in isolating certain specific processes in the organism, and attempts may now be made to conceive of these in terms of neurophysiology. The definition may thus be an indispensable means of isolating certain types of physiological processes. Before the definition is achieved we have to speculate more or less about the nervous system as a totality. Actually the pioneer research worker in psychophysics, Helmholtz, seems, at least implicitly, to have worked on the assumption that what was needed were the rigorous definitions of conscious elements. His requirement of rigor may explain why he would not call himself a psychologist. The endeavors of his assistant Wundt must have appeared quite amateurish to him. In Wundt's psychology, as in the later one of phenomenology and behavioristics, the rigorous definitions are lacking.

By defining a set of experiences by means of a set of antecedent conditions and a set of responses we have created a concept. We have defined a class of psychological events. I shall return to this conception of a class of psychological events in the next chapter. Here I would like to call attention to the fact that by our definition we have acquired some knowledge about the set of experiences. We have learnt to know the relationship of the set of experiences to two sets of observations. Thus we might state that we have obtained a concept containing our original set of experiences E plus some new knowledge. By relating our set E to still other sets of observations we acquire some further knowledge in our concept. As research progresses, more and more knowledge will be contained in the concept. However, it must be clear that the

31

concept will always contain the original set of experiences. Thus the psychological concept of hue will always contain a set of experiences of hue. Because some knowledge is acquired by the definition of the set of experiences it may be wise to have a denotation for this knowledge. We will refer to it as C. Instead of stating that E is defined in terms of A and R, we shall state that we have created a concept C which has reference to: 1. a set of experiences, E; 2. a set of observations underlying some set of antecedent conditions, A; and 3. a set of responses, R. We might accordingly redraw our diagram in the following way:

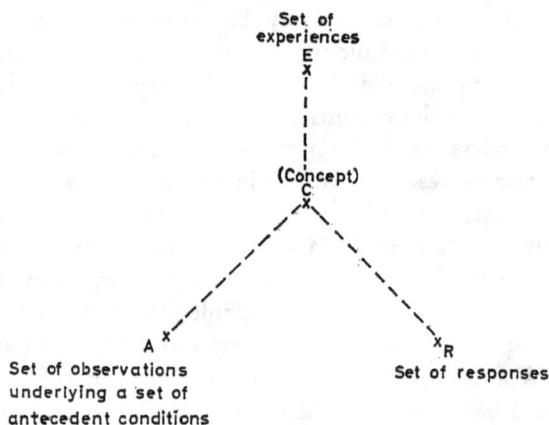

Set of
experiences
E
x
I

I
I
I
(Concept)
C
x

A x

Set of observations
underlying a set of
antecedent conditions

x R

Set of responses

Figure 4.

It follows from our considerations that the concepts at the level of analysis with which we are concerned must have a clear reference in three directions. In the last three chapters of this book various concepts used in the study of psychology will be examined from the point of view of this threefold reference. When this threefold reference is not adequate it will be seen that it is not possible to decide whether circularity, or empirically empty statements, are involved. I shall refer to sets of observations which are not related to each other by a definition as here described by the term 'isolated sets of observations'.

With reference to what I have called the first step in the

attempt at creating a scientific system in psychology we may define the task of the psychologist in the following way: a specified set E of experiences is to be defined by reference to a set of antecedent conditions and a set of responses. This definition I believe can only be accomplished by a discovery. Therefore, a scientific system of psychology must be established by a series of discoveries.

To illustrate the present conception of a scientific psychology in the area of perception we might state that the task confronting the research worker in this area is to define in the way outlined above the various aspects of our perceptual world, or what we may refer to as perceptual experiences, such as hues, brightnesses, saturations, glossinesses, insistencies and pronouncednesses of colors, pitches, loudnesses, volumes, smells, tastes, directions, movements, velocities, sizes, forms, textures, surfaces, appearances of figure-ground, of wholes, Gestalts, structures, thing-likenesses, of nearnesses, of indentities, of similarities, of objectivites, of realities, etc.

The difference between the present conception of psychology and that involved in the introspective and phenomenological approaches is found in the requirement that the experiences to be studied are not to be regarded as some sort of invariable element or as directly observable. Thus the sensations of introspective psychology and the wholes, or Gestalts, of the phenomenological psychology are to be introduced by reference to a set of antecedent conditions and a set of responses. As we shall see, this point has hardly ever been made clear in the phenomenological studies of perception, and, even if a number of the perceptual experiences, referred to as sensations, may be regarded as defined in the manner here required, there seems to be a tendency also in early psychophysics to conceive of the events to be studied as directly observable.

In retrospect it may easily be understood why the distinction between concepts and primitives tended to be wiped out in the pioneer work on perception. As will be emphasized in the chapter on psychophysics, the study of perception originated as an attempt at extending principles of physics to a study of problems in consciousness. The systems of physics are based on primitives made up of perceptual experiences such as hue, brightness, pitch, loudness etc. In a study of perception these perceptual experiences cannot be treated as primitives, but have to form part of concepts by being introduced by definitions. Thus in systems of physics perceptual experiences serve as primitives. In contrast, in a system of perception some perceptual experiences serve as primitives and some form part of concepts. This difference may easily have been overlooked. For this reason the tendency to treat the perceptual experiences to be studied as primitives may have been continued in the European study of perception.

I shall turn to the behavioristic conception of psychology. Some of the points made in the previous chapter will be further elaborated. The statement by Spence (1948) quoted in the chapter on history may serve as the point of departure for an analysis of the behavioristic position.

In other words, the events studied by the psychologist, Watson held, should consist in observations of the overt behavior of *other* organisms, other persons than the observing scientist himself, and not in the observations of the scientist's own internal activities.

Spence here emphasizes that the behavior observed must be the behavior of another organism. In discussing the definition of hue we have seen that the rigor of the definition need not be affected by the fact that the set of responses is emitted by the scientist himself. The fundamental problem is not whether or not the responses are emitted by another organism, but in what sense responses, or behavior, can be regarded as overt and not belonging to the scientist's 'internal activities'. This problem has relevance to the organism studied as a perceiving and thinking organism. In the following we shall assume that the responses are emitted by another organism.

The response reported upon by the observer is a conscious element, or experience, and the theorist has to treat it as an experience. The response as an experience is the result of some activity of another organism, but it is also the result of perceptual and thought processes of the observer. The theorist is ignorant about the processes underlying the response as an experience. He is thus unable to determine what is attributable to the activities of the other organism and what to activities in himself. If he attempts to relate the response to other experiences by means of his unknown thought processes he will, as made clear above, be unable to ascertain that he has solely assumed the occurrence, or existence, of his primitives. The behavioristic psychologist thus is confronted with the same problem as the introspective and phenomenological research worker. In making theoretical statements about his sets of responses the result may be that he merely merges himself into his world of perceptual and cognitive experiences.

The behavioristic psychologist might solve the problem of distinguishing between activities in his own organism and activities in the organism studied if he could base his theoretical statements upon events in the organism studied. Actually I believe this is what the behavioristic psychologists have been aiming at. However, since these psychologists take their point of departure in a response, or an experience, they are merely in the possession of an event in their own consciousness and not of what may be considered an event in the organism studied. A response emitted by another organism may be the result of an endless variety of processes in this organism. By relating one set of responses to another set of responses we may merely be relating to each other some sort of totalities of processes in the organism.

An event in another organism is necessarily a construction. Before the psychologist has defined the processes involved in his construction he cannot know what he is studying. His attempts at developing theories will be mere speculation. In order to claim that the psychologist is studying reproducible, or objective, events, he must be able to define rigorously a set of processes in another organism. To achieve this definition he must have available in addition to the set of responses: 1. a set of antecedent conditions, and 2. some processes to which he may refer in establishing the relationship between his set of responses and the set of antecedent conditions.

It will be apparent that the processes referred to, in order to establish the relationship between the set of responses and the set of antecedent conditions, must be conceived of in analogy with the experiences of the theorist. So we are back in the position stated by Mach (1886) that a psychological study of another organism can solely be undertaken by the theorist's taking the point of departure in an analogy to his experiences. This point is missed when responses are treated as events in another organism. Thus Tolman (1932, p. 3) in his treatment of purposive behavior in animals and men proceeded on the assumption that he need not carefully state the experiences underlying his analogy. The result was that in his treatment of the problems he merged himself into the world of unknown perceptual and cognitive experiences.

The examination undertaken here shows that in order to define an event in another organism we must be able to give a reference to: 1. a set of antecedent conditions, 2. a set of responses, and 3. a set of experiences indicating processes in the organism which may serve to relate the set of responses to the set of antecedent conditions. It is thus seen that the requirements of a rigorous statement of a problem in a psychology aiming at an objective treatment of another organism are the same as those of a rigorous treatment of problems in consciousness. Whether psychology is conceived of as the objective study of another organism, or as the study of consciousness, the essential point is to define an event, or a set of processes, in an organism.

As a result of the failure to distinguish between an event in another organism and an event in the consciousness of the observer the behavioristic psychologist has not realized the necessity of relating the set of antecedent conditions to the set of responses by experiment. In the chapter on behavioristics we shall see how leading behavioristic research workers restrict themselves to specifying the conditions under which a response occurs, and thus do not relate by a definition the response emitted to the organism studied. The set of antecedent conditions are merely assumed. It is when the problem of relating the set of responses to the organism presents itself that the theorist will meet the difficulties involved in the fact that the organism is a perceiving and thinking organism.

The tendency to base a psychological study on sets of isolated responses was introduced by Watson (1927) when he stated that psychology was confronted with two problems: 1. that of predicting the situation when the response was given and 2. that of predicting the response when the situation was given. The tendency to proceed by merely assuming the set of antecedent conditions has led to the broadening of the term 'perception' to include a variety of unknown experiences, or processes, and it has also resulted in the inability of behavioristic research workers to give a scientifically meaningful formulation of the problem of learning. To these problems I shall return in the last chapter.

In the definition of psychology as the study of behavior, behavior must necessarily refer to events or processes in another organism. Otherwise the definition is not meaningful. Behavior is then something abstract, a construct. In this sense behavior has reference to something vague and illusive. However, to the behavioristic psychologist behavior apparently has meant responses. It is suspected that these responses have been endowed with some ultimate reality. In an article on Watson, Bergman (1956) stressed the tendency in the founder of behaviorism to engage in mysticism. Even recently one of the staunchest proponents of behavioristic psychology, Skinner (1959), could report an instance of 'pure behavior'.

In retrospect one can only wonder why the study of behavior could ever be conceived of as an objective one. As conscious elements responses are hardly more public than a number of perceptual experiences. And a number of perceptual experiences are also, like responses, localizable to the space outside of our body. Thus, the color of a house, or the experience of the house as a totality, cannot reasonably be conceived of as less public than the locomotion of some organism in relation to the house.

Actually the tendency to conceive of the study of behavior as objective may rest on a confusion of objectivity in a scientific sense which refers to reproducibility of the events studied and the impression of objectivity inherent in our experiences of responses. To indicate what the impression of objectivity, or reality, may refer to I shall take my point of departure in some reflections of von Fieandt (1956). He argues that the impression of objectivity in perceptual experiences is enhanced the more sensory modalities may be assumed to interact to create the experience, and further that the impression is enhanced the more perceptual aspects are present in the situation. We may illustrate this point of view with the following example. When we are presented with some small color patch in a psychophysical situation, the experience seems to be highly dependent upon us as observers. The experience seems to be accompanied by an impression of a small degree of objectivity, or reality. This impression of objectivity appears to be increased if we introduce some texture in the patch. Further we may increase the impression of objectivity by having the color appear as belonging to an object. Still further we may increase the impression of objectivity by allowing the observer to perceive the object in a more complex spatial relationship. Finally we may allow the observer to touch the object and produce sounds by it. Now we seem to approach a maximal impression of perceptual objectivity.

To these speculations I would like to add that an even greater impression of objectivity seems to be attached to perceptual experiences of movements in another organism. The very fact that these movements are performed independently of a muscular activity of our own organism seems to endow them with an impression of objectivity. In general, the less an activity appears to depend upon ourselves as active organisms, the more objective the impression inherent in the experiences tends to be. Whatever the reason may be for the tendency to conceive of responses as representing objective events it must be emphasized that a study of behavior can only have a meaning if the term 'behavior' refers to events in another organism. These events are constructions, and cannot be arrived at by a study of isolated sets of responses.

The conception of psychology here advanced is in agreement with the behavioristic position that psychological concepts must be introduced by reference to a set of antecedent conditions and a set of responses. In this respect it is in agreement with Tolman's (1936) position that mental processes figure in a psychological system as intervening variables. Tolman's thinking about the intervening variable has been a major source of inspiration for the formulations here advanced.

38

However, the present conception differs from his inasmuch as it is required that the research worker does not resort to conscious elements in the construction of the system unless they have been rigorously defined by means of primitives. This means: 1. that the concept must contain specific reference to a set of experiences, and 2. that only one concept can be interlinked between one set of antecedent conditions and one set of responses. The first point implies that when the research worker studies another organism he must begin by making explicit the analogy to the experiences of which he avails himself. As previously noted, Tolman rejected the notion that the behavior of another organism had to be studied by analogies to the theorist's consciousness. As for the second point Tolman apparently did not feel it necessary to restrict to one the number of concepts introduced by one set of antecedent conditions and one set of responses. In the next chapter Tolman's conception of the intervening variable will be further examined.

The experiment

Psychologists have devoted little attention to the problem of what can be meant by an experiment in psychology. In the introspective and phenomenological periods the discussion was concentrated on the central theoretical constructs of the sensation and the whole respectively. In behavioristics attention has to a large extent been focussed on problems of theory construction on the advanced levels of science. Again, in this period the experiment received little attention (cf. Woodworth and Schlosberg, 1961, and *Handbook of Experimental Psychology*, Stevens (ed.), 1951).

In behavioristics the methodologists have tended to formulate principles by reference to theory construction in the advanced systems of physics. This reference to physics may have been very unfortunate for the advancement of psychology as a science. In the first place the preoccupation with methodological problems in the advanced systems of physics may lead the methodologist to overlook basic problems which characterize psychology as a science.

Secondly, the activities in which the physicist is engaged in developing his theory are enormously complex. The philosopher and the physicist, besides, may easily overlook essential aspects. As mentioned, behavioristics was strongly influenced by the science of science movement. To a research worker in *thinking* the idea of a science of science (cf. Stevens, 1939) appears most monstrous. More than 60 years ago Thorndike placed his cat in his puzzle box. We know that the cat escaped, but no one has so far been able to account satisfactorily for how it escaped. Apparently the puzzle box in which the scientist is placed is of an entirely different order of complexity. Before the psychologist can give a satisfactory account of the scientist's thinking, psychology must be on a very advanced level.

At the present stage of psychology it is hardly fruitful to conceive of the experiment as a means of testing deductions from theories. In the first place the theories will lack the rigor required in the making of deductions. Hull's (1943) attempt at applying the hypothetico-deductive method may be considered an utter failure (cf. Koch, 1954). It is not likely that another research worker would succeed any better in this type of endeavour.

Further, it is apparently very difficult to gain support for a theory by predictions. The psychological research worker is confronted with the problem of determining what can be meant by a prediction. Taking a pragmatic view of theory construction in science, a theory may be said to possess a high degree of usefulness when it makes possible a prediction of some unknown empirical relationship. The prediction may then be said to support the theory. However, if it cannot be made clear that a new relationship is discovered by means of the theory, no prediction is made and no support is obtained for the theory. In most areas of psychology our knowledge is so inadequately structured that we are hardly able to decide on whether or not a prediction has been made. The fact that a certain relationship seems to follow from some theoretical statements, or some model, does not ascertain that a prediction is involved. The theorist might have had in mind the empirical relationship which he purports to predict *before* he formulated his theoretical statements or introduced his model. If he cannot prove that this is not the case, no prediction can be said to be made. Support for a theory by means of predictions can thus only be obtained in well-structured areas of scientific research.

Even in the best advanced areas of psychological research it is difficult to ascertain the existence of a prediction. When, for example, the duplicity theory (cf. Saugstad and Saugstad, 1959) is examined from the point of view of discovering whether predictions have been made or not, it is difficult to arrive at firm conclusions. The empirical relationships covered by this theory may have been established independently of any knowledge of it.

Instead of regarding the psychological experiment as a means of testing deductions from theory, it might, in agreement with Stuart Mill (1843), be treated from the point of view of inductive inference. Such a treatment would not only lead us into the extremely complicated problems of inductive logic (cf. von Wright 1951), but it would also lead us to overlook the pragmatic nature of science. The experimenter is a discoverer and even at the low level of theory construction in psychology deductions are involved in experimental work.

In line with the author's conception of psychology the experiment will here be regarded as a means of establishing a definition of a set of experiences in oneself or a set of processes in another person or animal. The term definition is used to indicate an aspect of scientific thinking pointed to by Poincaré (1902). The requirements for a useful definition may help to call attention to some basic problems in psychology. This conception of the experiment advanced is pragmatic, the research worker being considered a hybrid of a logician and an inventor. Thus if the research worker, in his first approach to a problem area, has in mind a variety of events and is only capable of including some of these in his definition, he will still stick to his definition if it proves useful. To decide on the usefulness of a definition is a complicated task. However, a main point in scientific procedure is that the systems developed are abstractions. They never aim at covering all aspects of the particular case.

In the experiment, as conceived here, the scientist defines a class of events in terms of his two experimental variables. This means that the psychological researcher must be in possession of a set of antecedent conditions, a set of responses and a set of experiences, or processes, to be defined. Thus he may define a set of hue experiences by means of wavelength and a set of responses. This definition has proved useful, and as long as it does so, the researcher in the area of color research will employ it in spite of the fact that there may be experiences of hue not included in his definition. Another example from psychophysics is the researcher who defines a set of experiences of pitch by means of the frequency of sound waves and a set of responses to changes in frequency. The usefulness of the definition is essential. The definition is neither right nor wrong.

Since we, in the experiment, define a set of experiences or processes by reference to a set of antecedent conditions and a set of responses, it does not make sense to state that we have established a functional relationship between the set of experiences and the set of antecedent conditions. Thus, we cannot state that the set of hue experiences is a function of wavelength. What we have done is to define hue in terms of wavelength and a set of responses. Also, we must be careful in stating the functional relationship between our two variables. Thus, when we state that there is some definite functional relationship between a physical dimension, and a set of responses, it must be clear that the relationship is restricted to the situation where the set of experiences is defined in terms of S and R. Consequently, if the situation is changed, as in modern psychophysical scaling, the formula $R = f(S)$ becomes empirically meaningless. I shall return to this problem in the next chapter. The important point to note is that we are concerned with definitions and must be careful not to relate the experimental variables to each other without due regard for the set of experiences or processes to be defined, or to relate the set of experiences or processes to only one of the experimental variables.

The conception of the experiment as a type of definition may make experimental work seem prosaic. One may ask if this type of task does not also involve drama and excitement. The drama and the excitement belong to the experimenter's private life. As mentioned, the experiment rests on a discovery and the experimenter is a discoverer. However, at present we know nothing about the psychological processes underlying his discovery and we have to take our point of departure in the fact that some discovery has been made. This discovery implies that a certain set of events has a certain relationship to two other sets of events. In terms of this discovery a hypothesis is formulated about the outcome of an experiment. This formulation of the hypothesis is essentially of a deductive nature. The experimenter deduces certain consequences from his discovery. To illustrate this point we shall consider the definition of the class of events subsumed under achromatic contrast.

At some time, someone, possibly a painter, discovered that the brightness of a patch of color would undergo a change when it was placed adjacent to a patch of color of a different brightness. In terms of this discovery the experimenter advanced the hypothesis that the brightness of a patch of color will undergo changes when placed adjacent to color patches of different brightnesses. This hypothesis is of the nature of a deduction. The hypothesis is then carried to a test. Somewhat simplified, we may describe the procedure in the following way: one patch of color, P, is placed inside another patch of color, A, the brightness of which is varied. Now, differences are noted in the brightness of P when variations are introduced in A. Because this procedure brings in certain problems related to memory processes, a third patch, T, may be introduced. The brightness of T is matched to the brightness of P. In this experiment the changes in the color of A underlie the independent or systematic variable. The settings of the subject on the patch T, give the set of responses. In terms of this experiment we define the set of events, the set of conscious experiences as *contrast*, and we have experimentally established the concept of achromatic contrast.

In the above example the relationship between the set of responses and the set of antecedent conditions is introduced by a definition and not by theory. Thus, Helmholtz and Hering disagreed as regards the theoretical explanation of contrast, but they agreed on the class of events they conceived of as involved in the definition. Similarly, research workers have disagreed for one hundred years over the theoretical explanation of hue, but probably the majority of the research workers agree on the definition of hue. To give a third example, the research workers disagree on theories of pitch, but they agree on the definition of pitch.

With regard to the definition of achromatic contrast it may have been noticed that the experimental procedure involved one aspect not contained in our deduction. Consequences were deduced for patch P being placed inside patch A. No consequences were deduced for patch T used for the matching procedure. It was assumed that the settings in patch T would reflect the appearance of P. The tenability of this assumption may be doubted. Therefore, a number of new tests might be performed to clarify the implications of the matching procedure. As a result of these tests, the definition might be retained, modified, or discarded.

With these conceptions in mind we shall turn to the psychological experiment. In terms of our requirements for a rigorous definition it will be seen that a useful experiment is not easy to perform. In the first place it is frequently difficult to specify the set of experiences or processes which we want to define. The events we want to study are frequently not easily disentangled from larger complexes. We may fairly well specify a set of experiences of hue, pitch, brightness, loudness and other types of conscious elements dealt with in psychophysics. Specification appears to be more difficult when we turn to wholes or Gestalts. As regards learning, specification is apparently very difficult, and in other areas of psychology it may be even more difficult to specify what we want to define. It follows from our position that we will have no scientific psychology unless we are able to carry out this specification. It is by means of this specification that we are able to order our sets of observations.

As emphasized, the definition of one set of experiences in terms of a set of antecedent conditions and a set of responses involves a discovery, and it is usually difficult to achieve such a definition. In much research work in psychology, as we will repeatedly have occasion to observe in later chapters, only a set of responses is specified. Also it appears to be difficult to specify the set of antecedent conditions and the set of responses independently of each other. As we shall see later, in many investigations the two experimental variables are not distinguishable in terms of an operational analysis. It is very often time-consuming to find out whether or not the variables are distinguishable. With regard to the set of antecedent conditions these must at least be specifiable in such a way that some condition is either present or absent. Even this minimum requirement is not easily met with in psychological research.

In this treatment of the experiment I have insisted that one concept, and only one, should be defined by an experiment. A different type of concept from that described by Hempel

(1952) seems to be demanded. When Tolman (1936) had introduced his idea of the intervening variable, MacCorquodale and Meehl (1948) raised the question of whether or not the intervening variable might have a meaning in addition to that derived from the two experimental variables. My position will be that the set of experiences, or processes, must be rigorously defined in terms of these two variables. However, as mentioned in the preceding chapter, the concept created may be referred to new sets of observations. Thus, the information contained in the concept may be increased without interfering with the rigor of the definition. The concept created will still be an intervening variable and not a hypothetical construct in the sense of MacCorquodale and Meehl. Ginsberg (1952) has argued that the intervening variable seems to correspond to a scientific law, whereas the hypothetical construct corresponds to a scientific theory. The experimentally established concept apparently corresponds to a law.

By means of the experiment we have defined a class of events. At the level of research with which we are concerned in this book, this ought to be the definition of the class concept for psychology. The expression intervening variable is not appropriate. It will be seen that this class concept is not completely arrived at by the operational specification. The two experimental variables, but not their relationship may be operationally specified by means of the set of experiences, or processes. Thus, it is seen that a class concept in psychology cannot fully be described in operational terms. Bills (1938) made this point at the advent of Bridgman's (1928) operationism, but Stevens (1939) seems to have confused the issue. He cited as example what he called the class of horses. This is no psychological class concept. If Stevens had considered, for example, the empirically established concept of loudness, he would have discovered what I believe to be his mistake.

In the discussion of the experiment I have referred to some definitions in psychophysics, such as that of hue, pitch, and contrast. As previously remarked, this area of psychology appears to be further advanced than the others. In the other areas the experimentally established concepts are few. To illustrate further my conception of the psychological experiment, I shall examine some historically well-known investigations.

Imageless thought

At the beginning of this century Binet (1903) undertook some investigations on thought processes which possess considerable historical interest, since they represented the beginning of an extensive research activity lasting more than a decade and causing a heated debate, which may have inspired Watson to his revolt. The various investigations gave different results. On the question of whether or not the subjects obtained images on the presentation of some word, some reported that they had images and some not. These investigations were discarded by some since they did not reveal satisfactory uniformity in the results. Others have maintained that the results after all showed relatively good agreement. (For a discussion see Humphrey, 1951; Woodworth, 1938; and Boring, 1950.) Actually, whether or not the results agree in this type of investigation seems to be irrelevant. In whatever way the results had come out there would hardly have been anything to learn from them. Let us examine Binet's procedure, which is representative, even though it has been modified by other research workers.

Binet presented his subject with a certain word, for example horse, and instructed the subject in advance to say whether or not the occurrence of meaning aroused by the word at presentation was accompanied by the presence of some image. We will assume for the sake of the argument that the subjects participating in the investigations in Paris, as well as in Würzburg, Leipzig, and Cornell, all agreed that they had no image. In the first place, we note that no variations are introduced in the investigation, there is no systematic variable. It is, therefore, impossible to attribute any effect to an independent variable. More important, this investigation contains no specification of the set of experiences to be defined. There is no specification of the imageless thought. Consequently, we do not know what the set of responses refers to. It is also obvious that the opposite result would not have given us any important information. If all of the subjects had reported the presence of an image, it would not have been possible to define an image in terms of the procedure. The investigation would probably have been interesting if it had been possible to define the term 'image' more rigorously. There is hardly any discovery in this research, and there is no deduction. The investigation is carried out in terms of the trivial psychology of Wundt, concerning thought processes. There seems to be nothing here which may give us knowledge beyond that already contained in our everyday experience.

The cat in the puzzle box

About the same time Thorndike (1898) undertook some research on animal learning. He made a simple wooden box from which a cat might escape by manipulating some mechanism, usually a string. In manipulating this mechanism a door would open. A piece of food was placed outside of the box. On being put into the box, the cat would manipulate the mechanism and escape with subsequently diminishing time intervals. Thorndike drew a number of conclusions from this result. First, he formulated his famous law of effect, that learning was a result of the food given the animal after the leaving of the box. This so-called law has been criticized because the food was obtained after the cat had manipulated the mechanism. Actually there is no basis for inferring any effect from the piece of food since the food or the reward is not introduced as a systematic variable.

Thorndike further argued that the cat had learned to escape in a way which might be characterized as learning by trial and error. Actually, he was not in a position to specify what could be meant by learning by trial and error. His observations were so inadequate that the reader is not in a position to clarify the term 'trial and error'. Besides, Thorndike had, according to Adams (1929), made the fatal mistake of neglecting to accustom his animals to being kept in a box. The essential question is not answered: in what particular respect is the behavior of the animal changed? The set of processes which is studied is not specified. As a result, no systematic variation can be introduced and no conclusions can be drawn from the investigation apart from the one that the cat may be said to learn

48

to escape from the box at shorter and shorter time intervals; but this is hardly interesting information.

Thorndike's investigation appears to be devoid of discovery. It contains no serious attempt to state a problem. Thorndike is unable to handle his two central terms, 'reward' and 'learning by trial and error'. His research is no experiment, but a demonstration of his educational beliefs in learning by trial and error, and the school teacher's belief in the effect of reward or reinforcement. It is only in terms of these beliefs that a reader may conclude that the cat has learned by trial and error and as a result of reward.

Thorndike's investigation allows of no useful definition. It reveals the basic difficulty in the study of learning, namely that of specifying what can be meant by learning. Since the dawn of man's cultural life, it has been known that man and the higher animals are capable of learning a large variety of different activities. Therefore, the demonstration that an animal can learn gives no basis for a scientific psychology.

As a result of the inability of Thorndike and later research workers, such as Köhler (1917), Adams (1929), Guthrie and Horton (1946) and Spence (1951), to define the processes involved, there has been little progress in our understanding of what can be meant by learning by trial and error or by insight.

Tolman's (1936) definition of demand

As one illustration of his conception of the intervening variable, Tolman employed the following example. A number of rats have thoroughly learnt a maze. The rats are then divided into groups according to amount of food deprivation as expressed in hours since last feeding. Entrances into the correct alley of the maze are then recorded for each group of rats. Then, percentages are computed. The relationship between hours of food deprivation and percentage of correct entrances is plotted. If the relationship, as expressed by a curve drawn through the plots, is not distorted by variations in conditions which might affect the behavior of the rat, Tolman stated that we may assume that the curve expresses the relationship between an intervening variable (a demand for the given type of food) and the percentage of correct entrances. Tolman mentioned, as conditions which might affect the relationship, general stimulus set-up, number of previous presentations, other physiological drives, and specific heredity-, training-, and maturity-factors. We shall asume with Tolman that these conditions do not affect the relationship obtained. Still, the question appears as to whether anything is learnt from the experiment. Tolman seems to have overlooked the fact that before the experiment was begun the rats would have had to learn the maze under conditions of food reward. This means that we already know that there is a relationship between amount of food deprivation and entrance into the correct alley. We would not know the precise relationship, but the relationship is not clarified by the experiment performed, since it does not inform us why some rats entered the wrong alley. The rats might have entered the wrong alley for a number of reasons, for example, an innate position-habit might have been activated, learning might have been inadequate, or food deprivation might have had no effect. Since we are ignorant as to why the rats entered the wrong alley, we can hardly assert that we know more after having performed this experiment. We are not able to rigorously define a set of processes referred to by the term 'demand'. If we gave a definition, it would have to capitalize on our ignorance.

The Pavlovian (1923) approach to the problem of learning by temporal contiguity

Pavlov's procedure for studying learning seems to be superior in some important respects to the other ones developed. However, in the discussion of the Pavlovian procedure undue emphasis is frequently attributed to the introductory experiment, where it is demonstrated that salivation in an animal may be associated with the sound of a buzzer or some other perceptual event. There is hardly much to be learned from this introductory experiment. Aristotle expressed the belief that an important condition for the occurrence of learning was the temporal contiguity of the events to be associated. If Aristotle had been asked whether or not the animal might be induced to salivate at the presentation of a sound from the buzzer he might probably have replied with an affirmative answer, which he possibly could substantiate just as well as Pavlov. It will be remembered that Pavlov began his experimentation by presenting the animal with the sound of a buzzer, and that, as expected, the animal did not react to the sound by salivation. Thereafter, the animal was presented with sound and food in temporal contiguity a number of times in succession. After some fixed number of presentations of sound and food, the former was presented alone, and *now* salivation took place. By substituting other perceptual events for the sound of the buzzer, it was shown that salvation could also be associated with these. The inference drawn is that salivation can be associated with some perceptual event. However, the experiment does not give us any information as to how this association is established. The only systematic variation introduced is connected with the presence or absence of food. It is, therefore, not legitimate to draw any inferences as to how the association was established.

However, this introductory experiment has placed us in a position to examine experimentally some important conditions which might be relevant for an understanding of learning. In particular, the procedure seems inviting for a study of the role of temporal contiguity in the learning process. Aristotle was able to suggest his principle of temporal contiguity, but he was not in a position to establish it experimentally. Knowing that the animal might be induced to salivate at the presentation of a sound when this is repeatedly presented with food, Pavlov could proceed to introduce variations in the interval between the presentation of the perceptual event and the presentation of the food. The results made it clear that the animal, according to various criteria, learnt to salivate better, the shorter the temporal interval between the presentation of buzzer and food. The optimal interval turned out to be sufficiently close to zero to suggest that temporal contiguity is an important condition for the establishment of this type of learning (cf. Woodworth and Schlosberg, 1961). Still, we are not in a position to be able to make a rigorous definition of a principle of temporal contiguity in learning. An examination of the experimental variables will make it clear why this is so.

The systematic variable contains a reference to the presence of sound and food. However, our conclusion is relevant solely with regard to sound and salivation because these are the two events involved in our concept of learning by temporal contiguity. Therefore, the variable should refer only to sound. In other words, to achieve a rigorous definition we should be able to produce salivation in the animal in temporal contiguity with the sound. Pavlov had to produce salivation by means of the food. The inescapable question, therefore, is what role does the food play in the establishment of the association? Evidently, the food has some effect other than that of producing salivation. We know that when food is presented before the sound, in so-called backward conditioning, the effect of the temporal relationship is a different one.

As will be seen, we are not able to define learning by temporal contiguity by a reference to the two experimental variables. The definition we *can* make has to rest on theoretical speculations as to the presence of the food. As might be expected, a number of different theoretical formulations have been suggested with regard to this effect (cf. Woodworth and Schlosberg, 1961).

When we compare the Pavlovian procedure with that of Thorndike, we see that the former allows of specification with regard to important aspects, whereas the latter does not. In addition, the fact that Pavlov was able to orient his approach with respect to the already available knowledge about physiological reflexes makes his approach far more suggestive for further work than Thorndike's. Thus, in the area of conditioning a large amount of information has been collected, whereas the study of learning by trial and error, as instigated by Thorndike, has not led to a steady increase in relevant information. Still, the Pavlovian procedure hardly allows a rigorous definition of the type required by a scientific psychology. In the chapter on behavioristics I shall return to the problem of learning.

Psychophysics

Historically, the study of perception originated as a branch of physics. It was moulded in an attempt to extend the principles of physics to problems of consciousness. The designation 'psychophysics' thus gives a very appropriate description of the new branch of science. There was physics and there was the psyche. This origin of the study of perception, and thus of psychology, does not seem to have received due attention. Therefore, I will expand a little upon this aspect of the history of psychology.

The influence of physics becomes evident even in a perusal of some of the biographical material as presented by Boring (1950). Three of the leading research workers active in the 1860's, when this branch of science may be said to have originated, were physicists. There was Fechner, professor in physics for more than 15 years before his engagement in the psychophysical endeavor. There was Helmholtz, who became the leader of the institute of physics in Berlin, and there was Mach, who held chairs in physics for more than 30 years after first having been professor of mathematics.

The biographical material is certainly illustrative of the role played by physics. Turning to the type of systematic variables chosen, we find that they reflect the extension of principles from physics to the psyche. The same becomes evident when we examine the theoretical language.

By emphasizing that the origin of the study of perception, and thus of psychology, is to be found in physics, I have wished to focus attention on some central problems in the history of perception which otherwise might be missed. However, the role of physics should not lead us to overlook the fundamental interests in psychological matters among the research workers of this period. It is probably correct to state that Helmholtz, Fechner, and Mach were primarily interested in psychological problems. It seems also fair to state that Helmholtz devoted his best academic years to psychological research. Fechner embarked upon his psychophysical project because he was troubled with metaphysical problems of the mind. Mach approached the problem of mind from a somewhat different angle. He was occupied with the problem of how we could obtain knowledge and found a science when all our beliefs and activities were contained in our consciousness. Helmholtz was also absorbed by problems in the theory of knowledge, but his main interest seems to have been in the world of colors, tones, and space. The interest of these three great thinkers in matters of consciousness, in psychological problems, is central to their academic activities. Psychological reasoning is not thus introduced as a subtitute for the shortage in physiological knowledge of this day. In contrast to these three physicist-perceptionists, Hering may probably be characterized as a physiologist. One might suspect that he would have devoted himself primarily to the study of physiological processes if it had been possible for him to attack his problem of interaction effects in the retina directly. It is in the capacity of a physiologist that Hering became the permanent opponent of Helmholtz. Hering emphasized physiological processes, such as the state of adaptation in the eye and retinal interaction effects, which Helmholz tended to neglect.

Undoubtedly, much of the inspiration for the work of the physicist-psychologists came from the new physiology. Johannes Müller (1834—40), in his famous handbook, had collected and carefully systematized a wealth of information on the senses. One can easily understand what a tremendous challenge this systematized information might represent to a student trained in physics and interested in matters of mind. Physiology and anatomy served as an arsenal for models used by many of the research workers on perception of that day. It is in his ability to draw upon the systematized knowledge in the new physiology that Helmholtz demonstrated his wonderful creativity. It is interesting to note — and encouraging to an honest psychologist engaged in the basic work of collecting and systematizing data — that Helmholtz, the elegant model builder, devoted considerable time himself to the collecting and systematizing of data.

A creative research worker or thinker would hardly ever occupy himself with the concern of founding a new branch of science. This was left for the uncreative and unimaginative assistant of Helmholtz, Wilhelm Wundt. Nearly one hundred years afterwards, we may still ask how well grounded Wundt's founding of psychology was. The essential point is that the more formal founding must not be allowed to cover up the truly great psychological thinking of the physicist-psychologists from the 1860's.

Turning to the experimental designs of the pioneer research workers, one can see at once the influence of physics in the type of independent variables chosen. These variables were specified in terms of physical dimensions, such as intensity and wavelength of light, intensity and frequency of sound, area of planes, physical distance, position in terms of a geometrical system of space, weight, etc.

With regard to the introduction of the physical dimensions into the study of perception, it must naturally be kept in mind that physics has developed in the hundred years following the pioneer work in psychophysics. For many aspects of psychophysical work changes in theoretical conceptions in physics may not necessitate a reorientation with respect to the problems, but clearly the possibility of such a reorientation must be kept in mind.

In classical psychophysics the specification of the independent variable raises no serious problem. The psychophysics of Helmholtz, Fechner, Mach, and others was explicitly conceived of as a study of conscious experience. The procedure was usually straightforward and clear-cut. The psychophysicist was interested in knowing how perceptual experiences were dependent upon changes in some physical dimension. To define these experiences he had the subject indicate when a change in experience was felt to occur. These indications usually consisted of simple sets of responses, such as the single words, 'yes, 'no', and 'now', or the use of some simple signal. By means of the set of experiences, it was possible to relate the set of responses to the set of antecedent conditions. Frequently,

the designs in psychophysics resulted in experimentally established concepts rigorously defined.

As previously emphasized, the set of experiences, such as
those of hue, brightness, pitch, loudness, are not to be conceived of as observations. They are the events studied, the
experiences to be defined.

According to the conception of psychology advanced in
this book, a psychological concept must, in addition to a set
of antecedent conditions and a set of responses, also contain
a reference to a set of experiences, or processes. If no reference
to a set of experiences is made, I have maintained that we
are unable to ascertain the presence of some unspecifiable,
some speculative element, in our observations. I will now
illustrate this point with regard to the psychophysical experiment.

We will assume that reference is omitted to the set of experiences. We are then in possession of one set of antecedent conditions and one set of responses. The following problem will
arise: how can we relate the set of responses to values on the
physical dimension, how can we know that there is a relationship between our dependent and independent variables? There
is no rule for inductive inference which can tell us that there
is a relationship between the two variables. If this point is
not clear, our thinking about psychophysics will be confused.
Since psychophysics has been a part of psychology for about
one hundred years, we may have a tendency to take this
relationship for granted. It can only be taken for granted as
long as we conceive of psychology as the study of experience.
If we conceive of psychology as the study of behavior we are
in no position to infer any relationship. Suppose a person were
led into the laboratory and received no instructions about
what to do. He would hardly emit some specifiable response
when changes in physical energy were introduced. In order to
make him collaborate we give him instructions which are in
accordance with our experiences when confronted with the
task.

If we omit reference to a set of experiences, we have to
include *in the specification of our dependent variable* the
instructions given in the psychophysical experiment. In these

instructions the subject is strongly directed. He is first told that he is to participate in an experiment in perception, further, that he is to pay attention to some definite aspect of his perceptual world, and, finally, that he is to give a response of a specific type whenever he experiences a change in the relevant aspect of his perceptual world. The emission of the specified response clearly depends on changes in the perceptual experiences of the subject. We do not operationally specify these experiences in the psychophysical experiment.

In the instructions the experimenter conveys to the subject the type of experience he is interested in studying. The experiment rests on the assumption that the experimenter will succeed in this. It is important to note that the logic of the procedure is not changed if the experimenter uses an animal as subject. He has to give the same instructions to the animal, this time by a training procedure. To interpret the results of this type of experiment we again have to resort to our own experience. The question we ask in perceptional research in animals is the following: is the animal in possession of mechanisms which give it information identical or similar to that which we derive from our own experience? We study the animal by analogy. Thus, whether we perform the experiment with chimpanzees, monkeys, cats, dogs, pigeons, or insects, we still study our own experiences, and if reference to these is omitted, the procedure becomes nonsensical. We proceed by resorting to analogies with our own experiences.

The essential point in psychological research is not whether we use ourselves or other human beings as subjects, nor whether we use human beings or animals; the essential point is whether or not we are able to define rigorously a set of specifiable events by reference to a set of antecedent conditions and a set of responses. For this reason psychophysics is a sound scientific endeavor, while the behavioristic study of learning is not.

The study of psychophysics only makes sense when it is regarded as a study of perceptual experience. As a study of experience it has served well as the basis for the study of neurophysiology. Obviously, a neurophysiological study of the senses necessarily depends upon the study of consciousness. This was what a thinker like Helmholtz realized one hundred years ago. As a study of experience psychophysics can only be advanced by research workers taking the point of departure in their perceptual world. What is to be regarded as theoretically fruitful in psychophysics must be decided by reference to our perceptual world, the approaches which allow us to order this world being the fruitful ones. For this reason it is misleading when Graham (1951), in his discussion of visual perception, describes perception as a set of discriminations. Of course, the study of perception involves discrimination, but, obviously, not all discriminations are equally interesting from a scientific point of view. In the study of perception we are not interested in the discrimination between chairs and tables, cars and airplanes, horses and cows. The research worker in perception is interested in specific types of discriminations, namely those which allow him to create useful concepts for the ordering of his perceptual world. The discriminations in which the psychophysicist is interested can only be defined by reference to a set of experiences. Therefore, in his behavioristic fear of referring explicitly to perceptual experiences Graham gives a misleading presentation of what is involved in the research on perception. This attitude is also reflected in his discussion (1958) of the concepts of psychophysics. As I understand him, he asks whether the meaning of the concepts ought not to be determined completely by reference to the two experimental variables. Since we may want to leave open the possibility of relating the concepts to theoretical statements within other areas of research, for example neurophysiology, Graham concludes that it may not be advantageous to define the concepts completely through reference to the experimental variables. As I have pointed out, psychophysical concepts have no meaning if explicit reference is not made to a set of perceptual experiences. The question of the surplus meaning of the concepts is discussed in the chapter on the experiment, my position being that a concept can be rigorously defined in terms of the set of antecedent conditions and the set of responses and still be related to other concepts by theoretical formulations.

58

Our discussion of psychophysics emphasizes the study of consciousness as the basis for neurophysiological work on perception. Also, it asserts that a behavioral study of perception will be vague and uninspiring if the research worker is not always careful to relate his concepts to his perceptual world. The so-called behavioral techniques developed during the last decades may prove to be valuable, but a preoccupation with these techniques should not lead the research worker to neglect the source of all significant theoretical formulations in the study of perception. This source always has been and still is the research worker's perceptual world.

It follows from the above considerations that a functional relationship in psychophysics cannot be assumed to hold true when the instructions are changed. The set of responses emitted is dependent upon the experiences of the subject. The instructions specify these experiences. Therefore, when the instructions are changed, we cannot assume that the same set of experiences is involved. In other words, the concept may be a different one when the instructions are different. In the so-called direct-scaling technique of Stevens (1960) and others (Ekman, 1961; Goude, 1962; Eisler 1963) the instructions are continually changed, and, as a result, the set of experiences may continually change. There is no way of checking this fundamental point. Consequently, the procedure is no longer operational. The criticism of Garner, Hake and Eriksen (1956) is therefore justified when they contend that the procedure involved in the direct-scaling technique is not specifiable in operational terms.

The direct-scaling technique has been worked out without due consideration to the problem of the reference to experience. As a result, there is no way in which we can ascertain that the responses emitted have reference to the same class of experiences. Therefore, the responses cannot legitimately be related to each other.

I may illustrate this point on any of the types of experiences studied. Let us choose the one on which the most research has been performed, that of loudness. A number of methods have been employed. Stevens (1960) describes four: magnitude estimation, magnitude production, ratio estimation, and ratio production. To present my point of view it is sufficient to deal with magnitude and ratio production as one case and with magnitude and ratio estimation as another.

In the first case, a tone, l_1, of some specific frequency and amplitude is presented. The subject is then asked to produce another tone, the loudness of which constitutes some ratio or multiple of the first one. He may halve it, take one-third of it, double, triple it, etc. The following question arises: how can we know that the subject is able to stick to the experience of l_1 while he is making the production? Obviously, the subject is performing a complicated intellectual task. There is no way in which we can answer this question. It seems very likely that the experience of l_1 may be affected by the instructions. The experience of l_1 may thus vary as the subject is asked to halve it, to take one-third, or double it.

In the second case, again, a tone l_1 of some specific frequency and amplitude is presented. The experimenter instructs the subject that this tone shall have a certain loudness designated by some specific number, for example 10. Then another tone is presented and the subject is asked to estimate the loudness of this in relation to the first by giving a number. We see that the same problem is involved in this case as in the previous one. We do not know whether or not the subject is able to stick to the experience of the first tone l_1, and again there is no way in which we can know whether the subject does so or not.

The procedure rests on the assumption of the identity of the experiences of loudness of tone l_1 in the different tasks presented to the subject. This assumption seems dubious. As I have emphasized, complicated processes are involved, and we know hardly anything about these processes. The procedure clearly brings us back to a discussion similar to that carried on concerning the problem of imageless thought at the beginning of this century. Theories of measurement or the introduction of mathematics add nothing to clarify the basic problems.

If we examine the problem from the point of view of requirements for an experiment, we notice that the procedure does not allow us to specify the dependent variable independently of the systematic variable. Clearly, no experiment is involved. Stevens (1960) seems to argue that the procedure involves fundamental measurement. Junge (1965) has pointed out that this assertion is not valid. A simple way of conceiving the problem seems to be the following: what is the use of carrying out measurements when we do not know what we measure?

In a number of investigations by Stevens (1960) the relationship between the averaged estimates or adjustments by a group of subjects and the corresponding values of some physical dimension has been found to be describable by a power function, the ranges of the exponents varying from 0.3 to 3.5. Admittedly, this outcome is interesting, but as long as we do not know what is being measured in the various situations, the claim that the psychophysical function should be a power function is not warranted.

The direct-scaling technique is based on the assumption that the subjects' conceptions about numbers and quantities are in agreement with certain mathematical principles. It is assumed that the estimates reflect a use of numbers in agreement with a mathematical model. If this is not the case, the estimates will not give exact information about the perceptual experiences or the perceptual processes involved. For this reason an assessment of the direct-scaling technique is not possible before we know how the subjects conceive numbers and quantities. An application of this technique to problems of perception before we have adequate knowledge about our conceptions of numbers and quantities will lead to a confusion of theories of measurement with theories of perception.

Obviously, our conceptions of numbers and quantities raise intricate problems in the study of thinking. It is not to be expected that there should be one simple explanation of all the power functions obtained. However, in the two cases which seem most interesting to the research worker in perception, namely the results of attempts to scale loudness and brightness, the functional relationship seems explainable in terms of what I believe to be a general tendency in our dealing with numbers and quantities. In our conception of numbers we may tend to gradually decrease the interval between

61

adjacent numbers as the numbers grow greater. This would give us a distorted scale compared to that involved in the mathematics of the model, where the intervals are assumed to be equal. According to this point of view, the interval between 3 and 4, for example, is conceived of as greater than that between 1,000 and 1,001. Thus, in using numbers to indicate quantities, we may tend to use the numbers in agreement with a power function having an exponent less than one. Similarly, when we conceive of differences between perceptually given quantities, we tend to exaggerate differences between larger quantities as compared to smaller ones. According to this tendency perceptual impressions involving quantities will be systematically distorted.

The tendency to compress the scale is, I believe, a general one in our dealing with numbers and quantities, but it seems also reasonable to assume that in a number of situations this tendency will not dominate.

Thus, in situations involving pain and discomfort, such as in estimating the experience of an electric shock, or in situations involving efforts of various types, such as in the force of handgrip or in the lifting of weights, we may deal with numbers and quantities in ways different from that described. Also, the subject's estimation of the range of experiences involved may systematically affect the estimates and adjustments (Junge, 1965).

The fact that group data for a number of subjects are consistently describable by a power function thus cannot be taken as evidence for the point of view that perceptual experiences are scaled. Also, the fact that a group of subjects may consistently match experiences in one modality, for example of loudness, to experiences in another modality, for example brightness, does not give evidence for the point of view that perceptual experiences are scaled by the direct-scaling technique. If a group of subjects, or even individuals, can deal consistently with experiences relative to two different dimensions, for example amplitude of a tone and intensity of a light, it is not surprising that they can consistently match one type of experiences against another, as is found to be the case.

The fact that the assumptions underlying the direct-scaling

62

technique seem to be of a dubious nature does not, of course, imply a vindication of the Fechnerian (1860) or Thurstonian (1927) approach. The assumptions about a zero point as well as that of the additivity of just noticeable differences still seem to be dubious. When I have referred to quantities in the realm of perceptual experience, I have merely had in mind that we seem to be able to rank in a rough manner a number of perceptual experiences. This may be the only information conveyed more directly by our sensory systems. It should be realized that attempts to order perceptual experiences according to a model of a ratio scale may turn out to be a most unscientific endeavor.

As pointed out, the direct-scaling technique very likely involves complex cognitive processes. The perceptual experiences to be scaled probably involve relatively simple processes. However, in the attempt to scale them by the technique in question, the research workers may have come to deal with far more complicated processes. This is interesting, since the same development appears to have taken place in another area of psychological research where refined measurement has been introduced, namely in the study of intelligence. Here essential information on thought processes will probably have to be extracted from a study of the individual items of the tests. The tests for intellectual functioning are based upon extremely complex sets of observations, and, as might be expected, they have proved useful for an understanding of complex conditions, such as the role of social factors in the development of our thought processes. As we have seen, Binet (1903) was not successful in his attempt to experiment with thought processes. In the construction of his scales for intelligence he may be said to have left the study of the more simple and basic processes for more complex ones. A similar development may be involved in the attempts at ordering perceptual experiences by the direct-scaling technique.

Having considered some problems in connection with the experimental variables of psychophysics, we shall examine the theoretical language. Concentration of the early psychophysicists on the perceptual experiences called sensations is clearly a reflection of a preoccupation with physics. Psychophysics may be designated as the physicist's revisiting the realm of sensations. First, the physicist took his point of departure in perceptual experiences like hue, brightness, pitch, loudness, form, size, position, distance, and movement, etc., and proceeded to construct physical theory. Armed with the principles of physics and refined techniques for measurement, he returned to perceptual experiences. The early research workers had a familiarity both with the perceptual world and with the world of physics. They realized that this revisiting might result in new, refined knowledge. However, they do not seem to have realized that their return to the realm of sensations would necessarily involve a new way of treating sensations. They seem to have unwarily assumed that in a study of perception they could treat sensations in exactly the same way as in physics. By overlooking this difference they may have introduced a confusion into the study of perception. To understand the nature of research on perception it is essential to have clarified this difference. I shall now return to a point previously made (pp. 33—34).

Systems of physics and scientific systems of perception have the common characteristic that they are based on observational reports referring to perceptual experiences of sensations. This common basis was emphasized by the early research workers in perception. Thus, Mach (1886), in his consideration of the nature of science, took his point of departure in this common characteristic. However, neither he nor the other pioneers in the study of perception seem to have clearly realized that theories of perception must deal with concepts of perception and cannot be based merely on observations containing perceptual experiences. In a scientific study of perception, perceptual experiences must enter in two ways: 1. as the content of the observations, 2. as part of the concepts.

The perceptual experiences we want to study cannot be included in the observational reports. If this is done, they cannot be given meaning. The perceptual experiences of the observational reports are specified, but they are not defined. They serve as the primitives of the system. Physics avails itself of perceptual experiences as undefined terms. So does a scientific study of perception.

However, in addition to the undefined perceptual experiences, a system of perception contains the perceptual experiences defined in the concepts. In order to be able to study certain processes or events we have to treat these as something hypothetical, as something to be tested. The test is carried out by relating these processes or events to our two sets of experimental variables. Perceptual experiences or perceptual processes can form no exception to this rule of science. Therefore, we have to introduce the perceptual experiences we want to study as part of concepts. For this reason the perceptual experiences studied in perception are never observed. If this distinction between perceptual experiences as part of concepts and as the content of observational reports is overlooked, no scientific study of perception will be possible.

The subject in an experiment on perception, then, is no observer. There is thus no observer in addition to the one registering the set of responses. The subject is the organism in which the events to be studied are reproduced. The role of the subject in the experiment on perception is identical to that of an animal in a study of behavior. This point clarifies both the study of perception and the study of behavior. In the study of behavior the events to be studied are not observed either, they are 'inside' the organism. What is observed is the set of responses emitted. An essential point in the study of perception is that we cannot treat as directly observable what we wish to study. Sensations, Gestalts, wholes, etc. can never be observed if we are to study them. The fact that physics has availed itself of undefined perceptual experiences cannot be used as an argument for the legitimacy of this procedure in psychology.

The early studies in psychophysics made possible the creation of a number of experimentally established concepts. However, as mentioned, research workers do not seem to have clarified the distinction between a concept of perception and the perceptual experience contained in an observation. They tended to treat sensations as something to be observed, and later research workers continued in this line of reasoning when objecting that the observational reports concerning sensations did not exhibit a sufficient degree of intersubjective agreement. This criticism misses the point. In the study of perception, sensations cannot be observed, they must be defined. The point to be criticized with regard to the term 'sensation' is that it frequently lacks reference to observations.

The phenomenologically oriented research workers criticized the term 'sensation' from the point of view that it was an abstraction which was not adequate for a description of the perceptual world. They substituted the term 'whole' or 'Gestalt' for the term 'sensation'. However, they also overlooked the distinction between a concept of perception and an experience reported upon in an observation and persisted in trying to observe directly what was to be studied. The same seems to be true of Watson (1929). He shifted his interest from perceptual experiences to experiences of behavior, but he seems to have persisted in the attempt to observe directly what was to be studied. The key to understanding Watson and behaviorism is, I believe, to regard Watson as Titchner's successor.

We shall consider some examples of the treatment of the term 'sensation' in the pioneer work on perception. Wundt (1874) expressed a clear tendency to conceive of sensation as something not in need of an empirical definition, as something endowed with an *a priori* reality. He begins his discussion of the term by stressing the difficulty of isolating various types of experiences, but proceeds to state:

Diejenigen psychologischen Elemente, welche den Character einfachsten Erscheinungen zweifellos an sich tragen, sind aber die *reinen Empfindungen.* Wir verstehen unter ihnen die ursprünglichsten Zustände, welche der Mensch in sich findet, losgetrent von allen Beziehungen und Verbindungen, die das entwickelte Bewusstsein immer ausführt. In dieser Abstraction gedacht, besitzt die Empfindung einzig und allein Intensität und Qualität als nähere Bestimmung. (p. 273.)

The tendency to conceive of the sensation as some invariable element of consciousness is what makes the Wundtian psychology so uninspiring. The outcome of the investigations is known in advance. As we have seen, the Wundtian conception of the sensation as an invariable element is taken over in the direct-scaling technique of Stevens (1960) and his followers (Ekman, 1961; Goude, 1962; Eisler, 1963).

Helmholtz (1865—66), in his theorizing about perception, also overlooks the distinction between a concept and the undefined perceptual experiences contained in the observations. I shall consider as an example his treatment of color contrasts. He interprets the well-known experiment on colored shadows. Light from a candle gives the surface around a rod a yellowish appearance. The area covered by the shadow from the rod appears as bluish. The light reflected from the shadow area might have given rise to a gray appearance, since no predominance of short wave-length rays are reflected from it. If a reduction screen is used, the color of the area appears gray.

By varying the illumination from the candle, the concept of contrasts can be experimentally established. The concept of contrast as here experimentally established allows us to state that an area which otherwise appears gray, under conditions where it is surrounded by an area of some definite color, will appear with a color complementary to that of the surroundings. However, it must be noted that we have not defined the perceptual experiences of bluish color contained in the observations. It is to be noted that perceptual experience of a bluish color cannot be subsumed under the concept of hue, which is defined in terms of wavelength and a set of responses to changes in wavelength. The bluish experience is not defined.

To explain the results of the experiment, Helmholtz stated that since only rays of light associated with the experience of gray reach the retina and the subject still has an experience of blue, some unconscious inference must have taken place. The subject assumes that the surface as a whole is illuminated by yellow light. In order that some area can emit rays giving rise to the experience of gray, this area must have a bluish color since an object ordinarily appearing blue will appear gray in yellow illumination. As a result of this unconscious inference the area appears blue.

The speculations of Helmholtz derive no support from this experiment. The outcome of the experiment gives us no information about the nature of the perceptual experiences of bluish color contained in the observations. Helmholtz is not in possession of a concept which might allow him to account for the change in experience from gray to blue or in the processes underlying these experiences. In his theorizing, he can only give a reference to undefined perceptual experiences.

Before we finish these considerations on the theoretical language of the early research workers on perception, we shall deal with some problems connected with their treatment of the object. According to these research workers, the perception of the object was a result of associations between a number of different types of sensations. The object was a compound of sensations. As a compound of sensations, the object is clearly a construct. Therefore, the research workers, to be consistent, would have had to treat the object as a set of experiences to be defined and not as an observation. Obviously it is very difficult to reason in a consistent manner in accordance with this position. In his reasoning about the color of objects, Helmholtz seems to have confused the object as a construct and the object as an observed event. He raised the problem of why the appearance of the color of objects tended to remain constant under different types of illumination, and explained the invariance in the following way. We have had occasion to perceive the same objects under different illuminations. As a result, we learn the reflectance of the various objects. However, as Hering (1905—20) pointed out, we also, according to Helmholtz, register the illumination by means of the object. Hering seems to be correct in stating that Helmholtz is circular in his reasoning about the color of objects. The object is simultaneously treated as a construct to be defined and as an observed event. Woodworth and Scholsberg (1961) have taken a Helmholtzian position (as Katz, 1930, also did) insisting that the illumination can be registered independently of the objects. We shall not discuss this intricate problem here, but merely point out that the formulation, as presented by Helmholtz, does not seem to be adequate. The object is simultaneously treated as a construct to be defined and as an observed event.

Wundt (1874), too, is not consistent in his treatment of the object. Again, the object is regarded as a compound of sensations. Still, the term perception is defined by reference to the object. Since it is of interest to see how Wundt defined the term perception, we shall consider his definition in some detail. He first introduced the term *Vorstellung* which is said to be the image produced in consciousness of an object. Then he makes a distinction between a *Wahrnehmung* or *Anschauung*, and *Einbildungs-* og *Phantasievorstellung*. The former refers to what he designated as a real object and the latter to a non-real object. He also introduced a distinction between Perception and Apperception. This distinction refers to attention. Wundt here avails himself of a metaphor. Corresponding to the center and periphery of the visual field, consciousness was conceived of as having a center (*inner Blickpunkt*) and a periphery. When a *Vorstellung* reaches this center it is called an Apperception and when it reaches the periphery a Perception. Wundt's attempt to define the term 'perception' calls attention to a number of important problems, but he clearly fails to specify how these problems might be clarified.

Phenomenology

In the previous chapter I emphasized the notion that research work in psychophysics orginated in an interest in the perceptual world and that even physicists like Fechner, Helmholtz, and Mach were primarily interested in psychological problems. However, in the attempt to extend principles of physics to problems of psychology the research workers naturally had to limit the range of experiences which could be used as objects of study. What was to be studied was to a large extent determined by the systematic variables available. Phenomenology was primarily a reaction against the attempt to make the study of perception a branch of classical physics. In phenomenology the point of departure is taken in the perceptual world without consideration of, at least without explicit consideration of, how physical measurements might be carried out. Phenomenology, therefore, contributed to a clearer conception of what the object of study in perceptual research ought to be. The movement naturally led to the introduction of a large variety of interesting new problems in psychology.

The primary concern of the phenomenologically orientated research worker was the description of the perceptual world. Phenomenologists repeatedly pointed out the difficulties involved in accounting for the perceptual world in terms of sensations. More inclusive terms had to be applied; thing-likeness, Gestalt, whole, structure organization, etc. became slogans in the phenomenological movement. The new generation of research workers emphasized the importance of considering the relationship between our various types of perceptual experience. In this emphasis phenomenology has probably made a lasting contribution. The importance of paying attention to the interdependence of perceptual experiences had previously been stressed by Hering (1905—20), who had insisted, for example, on the dependence of object colors on spatial relationships, on contrast-effects, and on the effect of states of adaptation. Mach (1886) is also important in this connection with his inspiring treatment of the problems of color and form, and so is von Ehrenfels (1890) in his emphasis on what he called Gestalt-qualities.

Descriptions of our perceptual world like those of Merleau-Ponty (1945) and Rubin (1915) or explorations like those of Katz (1930) in the world of color, or of Tranekjær Rasmussen (1956) of complex perceptual problems bordering on the area of thinking are inspiring reading. However, it is difficult to assess the value of these descriptions. Even Gelb's (1929) systematic treatment of object color perception, or Koffka's (1935) treatment of form perception, the two peaks of phenomenological literature on perception, are not easily evaluated. A study of phenomenological literature raises the problem of how we are to decide upon the adequacy of the descriptions. As I have stressed in the chapter on history, neither the philosophers nor the research workers in perception have been able to specify what is meant by the phenomenological method. An analysis of this method will confront us with some of the basic difficulties in the study of perception.

A scientific system of psychology requires, I have contended, that we are able to define rigorously a set of experiences by means of a set of antecedent conditions and a set of responses. This leads to the conception of perceptual research illustrated by the diagrams in the chapter on defining psychology and reproduced here in Figure 5.

If we proceed in our description by only indicating a set of experiences and a set of responses, we are clearly only labeling our perceptual world, or we are merely enumerating perceptual experiences. The result will not be an ordered system of perception. The difficulty inherent in the phenomenological description is due to the fact that it is difficult to know whether or not the descriptions contain more than a labeling or enumeration of perceptual experiences. At best, phenomenology is a prescientific endeavor. This should not lead us to preclude that the descriptions do not contain relationships which may be transformed into the paradigm presented in

71

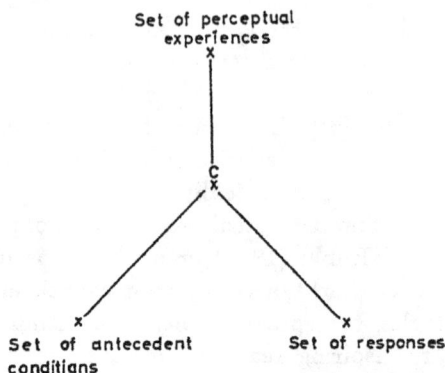

Set of perceptual
experiences
x

C
x

x
Set of antecedent
conditions

x
Set of responses

Figure 5.

Figure 5. Thus, we see that Purkinje's (1825) famous description of the relative brightness of hues approaches our paradigm. As is known, Purkinje noticed that with increasingly stronger daylight, the relative brightness of objects, having different hues, shifted in such a way that the objects possessing violet, blue, and blue-green hues were brighter under dimmer illumination, whereas the objects possessing red, orange, and yellow hues were brighter under stronger illumination. It later turned out to be relatively simple to change this description into an experiment where the suggested shift could be demonstrated.

When we consider the central terms of phenomenology, it will be seen that they are not empirically established concepts. The fundamental weakness in phenomenology consists in an effacing of the distinction between concept and observation. Terms like thing-likeness, whole, Gestalt, structure, organization are hardly ever used in the phenomenological studies of perception as empirically established concepts. Thus, to the scientific research worker in perception these terms raise serious difficulties.

If the phenomenologist insists that his terms are to be conceived of as the content of observational reports, he meets with the following two difficulties: 1. He will have to specify the conditions under which thing-likeness, wholes, Gestalts, or the like are observed. At best, this will give him some very

72

cumbersome observational reports. Most likely, he will be unable adequately to specify the conditions under which the observations were made. 2. He will place himself in a position where he is unable to test his notions about these terms. We cannot, of course, test assumptions about the perceptual experiences which we choose to include in our observational reports. These two difficulties force the phenomenologist to regard his terms as concepts.

If we conceive of the phenomenologist's terms as concepts, we will have to define them by experiments. Such a definitional process is, apparently, not easily achieved. Research workers with phenomenological orientations have constructed a number of demonstrations, but these are not sufficient to establish concepts of Gestalts or wholes. Some famous examples from the Berlin Gestaltists may illustrate the difficulties involved. The Gestalt laws of perceptual organization formulated by Wertheimer (1923) occupy a central position in Gestalt theory. These have been reproduced in a number of textbooks during the last three decades. Actually, these so-called laws are circular and empty of empirical meaning. For example, Wertheimer marked off a number of points on a piece of paper, as indicated in Figure 6:

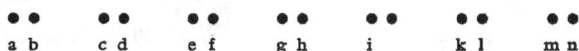

```
● ●    ● ●    ● ●    ● ●    ● ●    ● ●    ● ●
a b    c d    e f    g h    i      k l    m n
```

Figure 6.

The physical distance between points a and b, c and d, e and f, is shorter than that between points b and c, d and e etc. Wertheimer then formulated the following law: points which are near to each other tend to be grouped together. Thus, we have the groups a—b, c—d, e—f and not the groups b—c, d—e, or f—g. This is the law of proximity. It may be expressed in a number of ways. Points which are near (proximal) to each other form a Gestalt, a totality, a unity, or a whole; they are organized together, grouped together, belong together.

Obviously, it is possible to express what we perceive in different ways. I may state, for example, that I perceive a and b, c and d, e and f, etc. as nearer to each other than b and c, d and e, f and g, etc. Again, I may state that I perceive a and b, c and d, e and f, etc. as groups, units, Gestalts, wholes, or organizations, etc. I can express my perceptual experience in various ways. However, I cannot state, as Wertheimer and the Gestaltists have done, that the points that are nearer to each other form a Gestalt, a whole, or are grouped together. This is tautological. It is seen that the terms 'near' and 'Gestalt' (or 'whole') cannot be determined independently of each other. We have to specify them by the same set of observations. 'Near' and 'Gestalt' have in the Figure the same empirical meaning. What Wertheimer actually is saying is: points which are perceived as being near to each other are perceived in nearness to each other.

One may wonder why this tautology has not been noticed. The reason is probably that we confuse the two terms 'nearness' and 'physical distance'. Physical distance is not involved in the statement. There is only a statement about nearness. 'Nearness', or 'near' is a relative term which derives its meaning from a reference to some context. I may state that the two points, a and b, are near each other. I may also state that the moon is near the earth when I have in mind its distance from the sun. 'Near' is a term determined by reference to some wider context. For this reason Wertheimer's first law is empty of empirical meaning.

The law of proximity is frequently demonstrated in the following way.

Figure 7.

The points are perceived as belonging to vertical and not to horizontal lines. If I state the law in the following way: the points that are nearer to each other are organized together, I am making the same tautological statement as in the previous example.

We shall now consider the law of similarity. The law is illustrated by Figure 8:

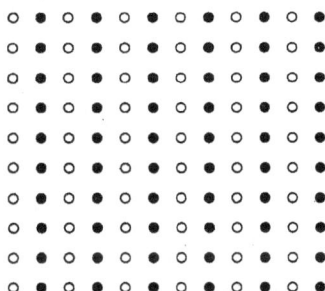

```
o ● o ● o ● o ● o ● o ●
o ● o ● o ● o ● o ● o ●
o ● o ● o ● o ● o ● o ●
o ● o ● o ● o ● o ● o ●
o ● o ● o ● o ● o ● o ●
o ● o ● o ● o ● o ● o ●
o ● o ● o ● o ● o ● o ●
o ● o ● o ● o ● o ● o ●
o ● o ● o ● o ● o ● o ●
o ● o ● o ● o ● o ● o ●
```

Figure 8.

The law is stated as follows: points which are similar, are organized together (are perceived as a totality, a whole, a unity, etc.). As in the previous case, the requirement for the statement must be that similarity can be determined independently of a totality, a whole etc. Again we see that 'similar' is a relative term. We can always find a similarity between two events. They may be similar in hue, brightness, saturation, size, form, or distance from the observer or another reference point. Thus, the term 'similarity' must necessarily be given a meaning with reference to some totality. When we state that some objects are similar, we are always stating something about the totality or whole. This means that in a given situation the meaning of similarity cannot be determined without reference to a totality or whole. Thus, this law is also tautological. Again, when research workers have not realized that this law is empirically empty, this is because the relativity of the term, 'similarity' has not been noticed. Similar may be qualified to mean similar in one definite respect, for example, similar in hue. I may then proceed to specify the term in question by physical measurements. This is not done in Wertheimer's demonstration.

The other 'laws' formulated by Wertheimer do not possess such a clear reference to his drawings as the two first ones. It is therefore more difficult to subject the formulation of them to an analysis. Koffka (1935) has given prominence to the law of 'good Figure'. The better — the more regular, the more symmetrical — the figure is, the better it forms a Gestalt. In Figure 9 A is a better figure than B and should make a better Gestalt.

A   B

Figure 9.

After examining Koffka's discussion, the question still arises: can Gestalt in these examples be determined independently of 'good figure'?

Rubin (1915, 1927) emphasized even more strongly than the Berlin Gestaltists, the necessity of an accurate phenomenological description in the study of perception. He also criticized the tendency among field theorists to engage in theoretical speculations. Still, when we examine the description given by Rubin of the appearance of figure-ground, we are not convinced of his having avoided circular statements. He enumerated a number of characteristics applying to the appearance of figure-ground: 1. the figure has form, 2. the ground does not have form and seems to stretch without boundaries in all directions, 3. the figure has thing-character, 4. the figure protrudes relative to the ground, 5. the figure is better remembered; it fills consciousness to a larger degree. The question arises: are these characteristics specifiable independently of each other? This question is not easily answered. All five statements may probably involve one and the same characteristic, namely that only one part of a perceptual area may have form at one point in time. Thus, it follows that the other area does not have form. Further, thing-character and form may be expressions of the same thing. Finally, the fact that the figure is better remembered may be another way of stating that it has form. The protrusion of the figure may also be implied in the concept of form. (For a discussion of this characteristic, see Woodworth and Schlosberg, 1961.)

A close reading of phenomenological literature would prob-

76

ably reveal a number of instances where it is not possible to tell whether the statement is circular or not. After reflecting upon the problem of circularity in phenomenological description in the study of perception, one wonders if this is not unavoidable. A characteristic of our consciousness may possibly be the following: *all conscious experiences present at one specific moment in time form a unity, whole, or totality.* If this should be the case, it would follow that at one moment in time we are not able to distinguish between parts and wholes in our perceptual experiences. All perceptual experiences would be dependent upon one another. Therefore, when we, at one point in time, characterize one part, we also,necessarily, characterize the whole. This would mean that from one perceptual situation we can only extract one set of experiences. Thus, we cannot extract both nearness and whole from Wertheimer's situation, nor can we extract both form and thing-character from Rubin's situation. This would mean that an accurate description of one situation, as required by Rubin (1915, 1927), will be a sterile affair since only one characteristic can be obtained. A useful description would then have to relate two different situations. These situations would have to succeed each other temporally. This seems to be what characterizes Purkinje's (1825) description. He noted differences in the brightness of objects as daylight increased from dawn to full day, i. e. at different points in time. It is also apparent that this requirement for a description brings us closer to the experimental procedure. In the experiment, changes have to be introduced, and the experimentalist is always searching for changes in some specific type of condition with which he can support his argument. In this connection we might bring to mind Helmholtz's (1909—11) suggestion (III, p. 21) that we obtain information about objects by a kind of experimentation, such as changing our positions relative to them and touching them in various ways.

I have pointed out how difficult it is to establish empirically the phenomenologists' terms of thing-likeness, whole, or Gestalt. In the phenomenological literature there are few, if any, experimentally-established concepts. The lack of concepts, of course, precludes theory construction. Actually, the difficulty of establishing the concepts of phenomenology might be circumvented if the Gestalt assumption, concerning the existence of an isomorphy between the physical stimulation impinging upon one type of receptors and the cortical processes, were tenable. If this assumption about isomorphy were tenable, we might develop concepts by reference to descriptions of the stimulation and to cortical activity. Actually, the assumption of isomorphy does not seem very probable (cf. Woodworth and Schlosberg, 1961).

The phenomenological descriptions in perception do not seem to have been fruitful for neurophysiological research. Not before a number of experimentally-established concepts have been created in a psychological problem area do correlations to neurophysiology become meaningful. As Tolman (1936) put it: 'A psychology cannot be explained by a neurophysiology until one has a psychology to explain.'

I have emphasized that phenomenology is at best a pre-scientific endeavor. By making it clear which aspects of phenomenology involve an inadequate conception of science, we may be able to bring into focus some essential problems in the scientific study of perception.

The phenomenologist frequently insists, in a one-sided way, on the reality of his perceptual world. By carefully describing his experiences, the phenomenologist believes that he may acquire new knowledge. He seems to overlook the conventional nature of science. In science we proceed by defining concepts in terms of specified sets of observations. Frank (1950) has given an exciting account of how the members of the Vienna Circle struggled to develop a more balanced view on the nature of science than that contained in positivism, how they became aware of the conventional nature of science and thus came to emphasize its logical aspects. Unfortunately, the logical positivists did not concentrate, as their inspirer, Mach, had done, on a study of perception, and they seem to have fallen victims to the fallacies of behaviorism in psychological matters. However, the logical positivists stressed the conventional aspect of science overlooked in phenomenology and, possibly, insufficiently emphasized by Mach. In a scientific study of perception the research worker has to proceed by defining his concepts in terms of definite sets of observations. A science cannot be established by labeling or pointing.

In the phenomenologist's treatment of perceptual experiences the fundamental difference between psychology and physics seems to have been overlooked. As it was emphasized in the last chapter, the systems of physics and psychology are similar in the one respect that they rest on observational reports referring to some type of perceptual experiences. However, a scientific system of perception must also contain concepts in which a set of perceptual experiences is defined. These perceptual experiences are not to be regarded as observations. Therefore, the treatment of the perceptual experience in phenomenology cannot be supported by reference to the procedure in physics.

The perceptual experiences we subject to study have to be endowed with properties which are testable. We test these properties by relating the perceptual experiences to sets of observations. If the outcome of the testing is satisfactory, we proceed to define a concept. The only assumption we legitimately can make about our experiences is that they exist. This means that the research worker in perception must learn to abstract himself from the familiar relationships of his perceptual world. Obviously, this is difficult. A characteristic of our perceptual world seems to be that some of its aspects obtrude themselves upon us with a forceful reality. It requires a high degree of creativity to find new relationships in the familiar world of perceptual experiences, and it requires clear thinking not to merge oneself into the familiar relationships when the problem formulated is analyzed. The difficulty may be illustrated by reference to our perceptual experiences of the concrete object. It obtrudes upon us as real and objective, but from the point of view of a scientific psychology we have no adequate theories to account for its appearance. We cannot even adequately account for isolated aspects, such as its color, shape, and size. Apparently, it requires considerable training to consistently regard the object as unknown. In the previous chapter we saw that Wundt, and even Helmholtz, did not seem to be successful in their treatment of the object.

The problems raised by the treatment of the object within

phenomenology has led to the introduction of a distinction between a distant and a proximal stimulation. Koffka (1935) introduced this distinction by reference to a table. The table, he stated, as part of the environment, may be referred to as the distant stimulation. For the excitation of the retinal receptors by light rays reflected from the table he used the term 'proximal stimulation'. This distinction may lead to confusion. In a study of perception the object represents the experience to be defined and cannot serve as a set of antecedent conditions. By referring to the object by the term 'stimulation', or 'stimulus', we may easily come to assume what we are supposed to demonstrate. This seems to be the fallacy which has trapped Brunswik (1956; Postman and Tolman, 1959). His treatment of what he referred to as the representative experimental design was largely based on a study of size constancy in objects. A subject is requested to judge the size of a number of different objects situated at different distances and perceived under different conditions of stimulation. Brunswik measures the size of the objects and their distances from the observer. He then proceeds to compare the judged size to the measured size of the objects and to the size of the retinal projection. The problem is what is judged by the subject. The subject judges an object situated in an environment. Therefore, the judgement necessarily implies a relationship between the object and its distance from the observer. This relationship is what determines the judgement of the subject. The investigation can give us no information about it. The projection on the retina does, of course, also involve a projection of the environment in which the object is placed. Consequently, we do not know what is varied in this study. It does not seem fruitful to conceive of this study as an experiment, and it is not easy to see what Brunswik's term 'representative experimental design' or 'ecology' refers to.

In passing, it should be noted that Brunswik (Postman and Tolman, 1959) was an advocate of the thing-language of the logical positivists. The assumptions underlying this thing-language may be of a dubious nature.

Brunswik became the adherent of an extreme operationism in the study of perception. The fact that he was able to measure the size of what he referred to as the object and its distance from the observer, does not, of course, mean that he was able to specify the stimulation serving as the antecedent conditions for a definition of the perceptual experience in question. At this point, mention should also be made of the term 'veridical perception'. An experience which seems to be in agreement with measurable characteristics is said to be veridical (Allport, 1955). If the term 'veridical perception' is to have any meaning we must be able to define the perceptual experiences underlying physical measurement and then make clear how these perceptual experiences form part of the concepts on which physical measurement is based. In order to contribute to the advancement of the study of perception Brunswik would have had to clarify what was involved in physical measurement from the point of view of psychology. By taking his point of departure in physical measurement he reduced the study of perception to a trivial affair.

An examination of phenomenological studies of perception makes the difficulty of distinguishing between a set of antecedent conditions and a set of experiences to be defined apparent. Therefore, considerable interest has been attached to the Gibson's approach (1951, 1959), which aims at establishing a psychophysical relationship between higher order variables of stimulation and perceptual experiences involving object qualities and various types of spatial relationships. Gibson's guiding hypothesis has been that perception is a function of stimulation. The problem is how to define stimulation so that we do not assume the spatial relationships or the object qualities we want to define.

Gibson regards the study of perception as being concerned with three different types of event. In addition to the perceptual processes and the stimulation described in terms of physical energy, he introduces a reference to the external environment. The problem presents itself as to how one can avoid attributing the relationships we want to study to the external environment. Gibson performs his analysis with reference to an optical array. The density of this array exhibits variations from place to place in the space surrounding the organism. We can thus specify a gradient of density.

In the definition of a gradient of density it will be seen that a geometrical description is involved. The geometrical description does of course involve spatial relationships. Therefore, Gibson may be assuming what he is to demonstrate. It should also be noted that his gradient of density raises intricate problems in cognition. His conception of stimulation assumes that the organism can attend to different parts in the visual field at the same time. The problem of attention becomes even more serious in his definitions of gradients where temporal succession of stimulation is involved. The organism must then in some way be able to accumulate effects of successive stimulation. Thus, Gibson's statement that perception is the function of stimulation will possibly have to be restated to read: perception is the function of perception.

Behavioristics

The behavioristic revolution led to a widening of the range of research interests, to inspiring reformulations of psychological problems, and to invigorating attacks on methodological issues. However, in the eagerness to open up new areas of research and in the impatient effort to push psychology along to the level of the advanced sciences, basic assumptions underlying the behavioristic movement were left unexamined.

In the chapter discussing the requirements for a scientific psychology it was pointed out that behavioristic psychology had failed to distinguish between an event in another organism and an event in the consciousness of the observer and the theorist. The response may be considered an event in the latter, but not in the former sense. I shall examine this distinction further.

By the rule of intersubjective agreement we may ascertain that a response is a reproducible, or repeatable, event. However, it must be clear that it is reproducible solely as a conscious element, or an experience, and cannot be treated as an event in another organism. If the experience of a response is subjected to study, it must be investigated in a manner similar to that in which perceptual experiences as, e.g., hue, figure-ground and thing-likeness are studied. Actually, From (1953) has carried out investigations on the experience of responses, or behavior.

When the response is regarded as an experience, a set of antecedent conditions to this experience can meaningfully be asked for. If a new set of responses can be found which can be utilized as the primitives, the experience of the response may be defined by means of the set of antecedent conditions and the new set of responses.

In contrast, when the response is regarded as an event which is to characterize another organism, it is not scientifically meaningful to ask for a set of antecedent conditions. We cannot know whether or not the set of responses refers to reproducible events in the organism studied. By merely specifying operationally the conditions under which the observational reports are to be made, we have not ascertained that we are dealing with reproducible events in another organism. Experiments must be performed which relate the set of responses to the organism studied. These experiments are lacking in behavioristic psychology. By regarding the response as an event in the organism studied, the organism is not treated as a perceiving and thinking organism.

A response may be the result of a wide variety of different processes of a psychological and physiological nature in the organism emitting it. The research worker who makes his point of departure a set of responses, must necessarily engage in extensive speculations in his attempt to relate the responses to the organism. He will have to refer to the experimental situation as some environmental total and to the organism as some psychological or physiological total. The attempts at constructing systems in this way will be lacking not only in rigor, but also in creativity, because no meaningful problems can be formulated.

When it is realized that a response cannot be regarded as a reproducible event in another organism, it will be seen that the stimulus-response approach of behavioristic psychology is not a meaningful one. An event in another organism is a construction. When it can be ascertained by experiment that a set of processes is reproducible, we may subject it to study. To ascertain that the processes are reproducible we must be able to define them by means of a set of antecedent conditions and a set of responses. In this definition the set of responses serve as primitives. It does not make sense to ask for a set of antecedent conditions to a set of primitives. Actually when we ask for a set of antecedent conditions (or for what has been referred to as a stimulus) to a set of responses, the primitives must necessarily also serve as concepts. This is the basic confusion in behavioristic psychology.

To show how the founder of behaviorism, Watson, failed to distinguish between an event in the organism studied and an event in his own consciousness, two central passages will be examined. In introducing the term 'stimulus', Watson (1929, p.5) stated:

Behavioristic psychology attempts to formulate, through systematic observation and experimentation, the generalizations, laws and principles which underlie man's behavior. *When a human being acts — does something with arms, legs or vocal cords — there must be an invariable group of antecedents serving as a 'cause' of the act. For this group of antecedents the term situation or stimulus is a convenient term.*

This statement by Watson has apparently been accepted as self-evident by behavioristic psychologists. As we have seen, it is not meaningful because the occurrence of movements by another organism, by arms, legs, or vocal cords, cannot be regarded as reproducible events in that organism. It is seen that Watson in formulating the problem of psychology is neglecting either to specify the reference to a set of responses which make up the primitives, or to specify a set of processes to be defined.

We shall also consider the introduction of the term 'response' (pp. 11, 12):

The general nature of response. — In a similar way we employ in psychology the physiological term 'response', but again we must slightly extend its use. The movements which result from a tap on the patellar tendon, or from stroking the soles of the feet are 'simple' responses which are studied both in physiology and in medicine. In psychology our study, too, is sometimes concerned with simple responses of these types, but more often with several complex responses taking place simultaneously. In the latter case we sometimes use the popular term 'act' or adjustment, meaning by that that the whole group of responses is integrated in such a way (instinct or habit) that the individual does something which we have a name for, that is 'takes food', 'builds a house', 'swims', 'writes a letter', 'talks'.

Apparently Watson did not realize what an enormously complicated problem he raised for the psychologist by this statement. If the response is to be related to the organism studied, it must serve as a primitive in the system. This means that together with a set of antecedent conditions it must serve as a

85

means of defining a set of processes. It is difficult to conceive of processes which may be defined by reference to sets of responses like 'house-building' and 'letter-writing'.

In passing it should be noted that in the physiological reflex to which Watson makes reference, a set of antecedent conditions, and a set of responses as well as indications of a set of physiological processes are available. The reflex may be considered a reproducible event in another organism.

The failure to distinguish between an event in the organism studied and an event in the consciousness of the observer and theorist, is revealed when central passages from the leading behavioristic psychologists are examined. Since Hull (1943) may be regarded as the most influential of the psychologists of the behavioristic orientation, a central passage in his writings will be chosen for examination, but it must be underlined that examinations of the writings of Spence (1951), Guthrie (1959), Estes (1959), Tolman (1932, 1959), and Skinner (1938, 1959) will reveal the same basic confusion.

In what Hull calls Demonstration Experiment I a rat is placed in a box so constructed that to avoid a shock it must leap a barrier. The details of the apparatus need not concern us here. We shall just note that the box has a glass ceiling permitting a view of the interior of the box and that the floor is made up of irons bars which can be electrically charged. The box is divided into two compartments by a barrier which can be leapt by the rat. The rat is placed in one compartment and after some interval of time the floor is electrically charged. After the onset of the current the behavior of the rat is described by Hull in the following way:

The animal's behavior changes at once, in place of the deliberate exploratory movements it now displays an exaggeratedly mincing mode of locomotion about the compartment interspersed with occasional slight squeaks, biting of the bars which are shocking its feet, defecation, urination and leaps up the walls. These reactions are repeated in various orders and in various parts of the compartment: sometimes the same act occurs several times in succession, sometimes not. After five or six minutes of this variable behavior one of the leaps carries the animal over the barrier upon the uncharged grid of the second compartment.

On the basis of this description Hull designated as responses: 1. the rat's leaping against the walls of the apparatus (R_1), 2. the rat's squeaking (R_2), 3. the rat's biting the floor bars (R_3), 4. the rat's leaping the barrier (R_4). In order to relate these four different responses to the organism (the rat) Hull would have had to proceed in the following way. For each type of response he would have to specify a set of processes and a set of antecedent conditions. Then he would have to demonstrate by experiment that each set of processes was definable by means of its set of antecedent conditions and its type of response. By means of four different experiments the four types of responses, R_1, R_2, R_3, and R_4, would have to be related to the organism.

Hull does not follow this procedure. He restricts himself to asserting that there would have to be sets of antecedent conditions producing the four types of responses. Thus he states that the rat would receive a stimulation (S_A) when leaping against the wall, a stimulation (S_A') when sqeaking, S_A'' when biting the metal bars, and S_A''' when leaping the barrier. In this statement Hull apparently proceeds on the following assumption: when behavior is registered, a set of antecedent conditions must also be available. The assumption is not tenable, because it is not known whether or not the four types of responses represent reproducible events in terms of the organism studied.

It is seen that Hull — and the same is true of the other leading behavioristic psychologists — begins the theorizing before the events to be studied have been defined. The result must necessarily be confusion. What Hull further wrote could only add to the confusion, and I shall stop the examination at this point. Hull proceeded in his theory construction to a large extent on the basis of notions about science developed by the logical positivists. Koch (1954) carried out a detailed and extensive analysis of Hull's system and demonstrated how he fell short of meeting the standards set up by logical positivism. Actually most of this discussion may be considered as irrelevant to the present stage of development of psychology as a science.

An examination of Hull's procedure reveals, as we have seen, that he restricted himself to an operational definition when the rigor of science would require a definition by experiment. Hull specified the physical characteristics of the cage, such as its size, color, illumination, and the material of which it was made. This is a specification in relation to the observer and the theorist and not in relation to the organism studied. What here is specified are the conditions under which the observer is to make his report. So what is specified is the occurrence of the response in the consciousness of the observer and the theorist. As mentioned, the same procedure is found in other leading behavioristic thinkers.

By this operational specification the theorist is obviously in the possession of a set of observations. But it must be noted that this set of observations is very vaguely specified. Thus Hull would have to state that in his box a rat would leap the barrier in, say, a time interval of from 0—5 minutes. The specification of the occurrence of the rat's jumping to the wall would have to be even vaguer. Here Hull would have to state that a certain percentage of a certain number of rats would jump to a wall, say, within a time interval of 0—5 minutes. With regard to both sets of observations Hull would have to disregard the other types of responses emitted by the rat, such as the squeaking, the biting of the floor bars, etc. Thus, the order in which the responses were emitted would have to be disregarded.

What must be clear is that the type of operational specifications undertaken by behavioristic psychologists will result in observational reports of a very complex nature. Apparently the following rule must hold true: the more complex the experiences making up the primitives of the observational reports, the less rigorous will be the definitions achieved by means of the observations. The attempt of behavioristic psychology to avoid a study of perceptual and thought mechanisms of the organism studied must necessarily lead to a loss in rigor. The question presents itself: is it possible to deal with basic psychological mechanisms when the research worker takes his point of departure in observational reports of such a complicated nature as those used by behavioristic psychologists. Here (Hull, 1943; Spence, 1951; Guthrie, 1959; Skinner, 1938; Estes, 1959;) the observational reports contain reference to complicated relationships such as those of an animal's locomotion in relation to objects (walls, bars, barriers, floor bars, etc.). Thus we have seen that Hull can only make a vague reference to the physical energy activating the sensory systems of the animal when placed in the box. This makes it difficult to distinguish between the effect of the current when the floor-grid is electrically charged and the effect of the other types of physical energy. In Hull's system the electric current has reference to a set of antecedent conditions which is to be distinguished from the set of antecedent conditions that are made up of the other types of physical energy. Demonstration Experiment I refers to a learning process. As a result of a repeated presentation of the rat in the box under the condition when the floor-grid is electrically charged, the rat will leap the barrier after shorter and shorter time intervals. Apparently the concept of learning can here merely refer to some sort of environmental total in which is placed an organism conceived of as some psychological total.

The problem of learning will be examined more systematically. Behavioristic psychology, we have seen, takes its point of departure in the specification of a set of responses. In line with this point of departure, learning is conceived of as involving changes in responses, in performance, not as involving changes in sets of defined processes (cf. Hilgard, 1956; Spence, 1951; Woodworth and Schlosberg, 1961). This point of departure cannot lead to an adequate conception of learning. Learning concerns changes in processes in an organism. By means of a specification of a set of responses it is not possible to define a set of processes in another organism. To arrive at a fruitful conception of learning the point of departure must be taken in what may be regarded as a reproducible event in an organism. The previous considerations have led us to conceive of a reproducible event in an organism as a set of processes rigorously defined by means of a set of antecedent conditions and a set of responses. Consequently the point of departure must be taken in a set of defined processes. It must then be shown that this set of defined processes can be changed into another set of defined processes. The problem of learning concerns how this change is brought about. To formulate a problem in learning, the research worker must be in the possession of two different sets of defined processes. Then he must show that one set of processes can be changed into the other by

89

some experimental procedure involving some specified type of stimulation. The situation may be diagramatically presented in the following way:

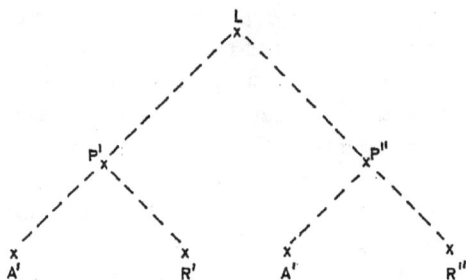

Figure 10.

In Figure 10, P' represents a set of processes to be defined by means of a set of antecedent conditions A' and a set of responses R'. P'' represents another set of processes to be defined in terms of A' and a new set of responses R''. L represents a set of processes activated by the experimental procedure and affecting the change of P' into P''.

It will be understood that L, learning, will have to represent a very complicated set of processes. At the present stage of knowledge it is even difficult to imagine such a set of processes. In this examination I shall merely be dealing with the requirement that two different sets of defined processes must be available. Not before two such sets are available can a problem of learning be fruitfully attacked.

When the point of departure is taken in a set of processes in an organism, it will be seen that learning must involve modifications of existing processes. Learning cannot be the result of the creation of new processes independently of already existing processes. In contrast, when the point of departure is taken in a set of responses, one might be led to assume some sort of zero performance in instances where the response is not emitted. Behavioristic studies of learning reveal a tendency to conceive of learning in this way. Hilgard (1956) suggested that learning should be conceived of as 'the process by which an activity originates.' The expression that an activity originates may be unfortunate because what may be designated as a new activity must necessarily involve a modification of some already existing activity. In a study of learning the existing activity must not be neglected, as it frequently is.

The requirement for a formulation of a problem in learning will be illustrated by the Pavlovian (1923) approach. The great merit of this approach is found in the fact that the point of departure is taken in one set of processes which may be definable. The processes involved in salivation to food placed in the mouth of an organism is at least approximately definable by means of a set of antecedent conditions and a set of responses. These processes will correspond to our set P'', the antecedent conditions being food in the mouth and the set of responses the secretion of saliva. By the experimental procedure another set of processes, P', is changed into the set involved in the salivary reflex. The weakness in the Pavlovian formulation of the problem of learning stems from the fact that it is difficult to define the set of processes, P', being changed into the set P''. Before the problem of learning can be formulated these processes must be defined. Thus if the animal is to be trained to produce salivation to the sound of a buzzer, the processes activated by the sound of the buzzer must be defined. At an early stage in the ontogenetic development of an organism these processes might possibly be defined by reference to responses involved in the so-called orienting reflexes. At later stages in the ontogenetic development it is extremely difficult to define the processes involved on the presentation of the buzzer. Evidently sound is associated with an innumerable variety of processes in the animal. What is particularly important in this procedure of classical conditioning is the fact that shortly after birth, sound and food may be associated in a number of ways. The fact that the organism does not salivate when the buzzer is presented until food and buzzer have been presented simultaneously, does not, of course, warrant the conclusion that sound and food have not previously been associated.

Under the assumption that the set of processes activated by the sound of the buzzer might be rigorously defined, we might study how this set, P', was changed into set P''. The study of this change would be a study of learning. In this connection it

91

should be noted that the Pavlovian approach meets with the difficulty that the first set of processes, whatever they are, are not changed into processes which are identical to those involved in the salivary reflex (cf. Woodworth and Schlosberg, 1961). At present it may still be difficult to conceive of the changes involved in a fruitful manner when set P' is changed into set P''.

The study by Thorndike (1898) previously commented upon (p. 48) will be considered next. Here it will be seen that the point of departure is not taken in a set of definable processes. The processes having reference to the successful manipulation of the string, or the other types of mechanisms opening the door, are unknown. Thorndike has restricted himself to a vague specification of the conditions under which this response will occur. The set of antecedent conditions which might be used to define the processes is not known.

Turning to the problem of the definition of the processes activated in the cat on its first entering of the box, we lack a set of antecedent conditions to achieve this definition. Also, the set of responses to be used in the definition is inadequately specified. Thorndike maintained that the cat emitted certain types of responses upon entering the box. Adams (1929) in repeating the study, reported what appears as quite another type of responses. On the basis of the description of the box and of the cat's behavior we can merely advance vague speculations concerning the set of processes activated in the cat when the training procedure is introduced.

Speculating about the possible antecedent conditions to which the cat's responses had reference, it seems reasonable to assume that these would have to be specified in terms of: 1. physical energy activating the cat's sensory organs while it was staying in the box, 2. physiological conditions influencing the activity level of the cat. With regard to point 1, the physical energy activating the cat's sensory organs can only be roughly indicated by reference to the characteristics of the box, such as its size, color, type of material, etc. However, no description can be given of the box in relation to the cat. This is the description we would need. To accomplish this description a number of experiments would have to be performed. Since these experiments have not been carried out, the box can only be described as making up some type of environmental total for the organism being studied. As we have emphasized, this vague description is characteristic of behavioristic studies of learning. It should be noted that the vague reference to the situation as a totality implies that we are merely able to refer to some sort of totality of processes in the cat.

Even if we were in possession of an adequate description of the box as related to the cat, we would hardly be able to control its behavior in an adequate way by variations of the physical energy, by variations in the immediate stimulation. Thus we might probably vary the color of the box, its illumination, the texture of the material in the floor and walls, and within certain limits its size, without achieving what may be regarded as essential modifications in the types of responses emitted.

Turning to the second type of conditions determining the cat's behavior, the physiological conditions, we could obviously change the responses by introducing variations in the nutritional state of the cat; but it is reasonable to believe that introduction of changes in physiological conditions in accordance with our present knowledge would not give us adequate control over the responses emitted by the cat.

It also seems safe to conclude that a combination of sets of antecedent conditions in terms of physical energy and physiological states would not give us adequate control over the cat's behavior. Obviously, to control the cat's behavior in the box in an adequate way we would have to go beyond the situation as defined in terms of physical energy and physiological conditions. The cat's behavior would also be dependent upon innate behavior tendencies as well as upon effects of stimulation received in previous situations. Thus, to define the set of processes in the cat, we would have to know its prior history. This means that we are not able to define learning by reference to the box and the responses emitted.

The effect of past stimulation obviously raises the problem of thinking. If past stimulation is to have an effect, the present stimulation must in some way be similar to the past stimulation. If we state that this similarity is a result of learning, we are merely pushing the problem backwards. At some stage in the study of learning we must necessarily be able to determine what can be meant by similarity between two stimulations specified in terms of distinguishable characteristics. Similarity, like any other psychological concept, must be determined by reference to the organism studied. As an example of an attempt at investigating the problem of similarity may be mentioned the writer's (Saugstad, 1955, 1958) research on problem-solving in humans. In these studies no rigorous definitions are achieved, but they indicate that a human subject will tend to emit a certain specifiable response over a wide variety of situations. Before the problem of learning can be efficiently attacked, psychology must have accumulated extensive knowledge about the problem of similarity. In order to formulate problems of learning psychology must first have clarified a variety of problems in thinking.

Due to the failure of the behavioristic psychologists to distinguish between an event in another organism and an event in their own consciousness, the inadequacies of Thorndike's procedure were not noticed. Research workers continued to specify sets of responses while neglecting the definition of processes. I have already pointed out how Hull neglected this problem in introducing his box for the study of the learning of the rat, and Spence (1951) endorsed Hull's procedure. Actually research workers like Skinner (1938) and Guthrie and Horton (1946) molded their procedure on the one presented by Thorndike. The boxes used by these research workers may be regarded as modifications of the Thorndike box.

As made clear above, early behavioristic research workers like Hull, Spence, Guthrie and Skinner may be said to have proceeded in their research on the assumption that problems of perception might be circumvented. After the Second World War the interest in perceptual problems was revived. However, in the approach to the problems the new research was influenced by behavioristic thinking. Behavioristic psychology, I have maintained, is characterized by the failure to distinguish between an event in the organism studied and an event in the consciousness of the observer and the theorist. As a result of this failure behavioristic psychologists have tended to take their point of departure in isolated sets of responses.

The tendency to take the point of departure in isolated sets of responses was carried over to the new research in perception. Reference to perceptual experience was indeterminate and so was the reference to the set of antecedent conditions. The result was that the term 'perception' was made to include wide varieties of psychological processes, and thus tended to be synonymous with the term psychology. Expressions of this tendency are found in the two symposia on personality, motivation, and perception (Bruner and Krech, eds., 1949; Blake and Ramsay, eds., 1951; Allport, 1955; Solley and Murphy, 1960). Even a research worker like Graham (1951), oriented strongly towards psychophysics, extended the term to cover a variety of experimental situations. Previously we have seen that Stevens (1960) and research workers on the direct-scaling technique probably unwarily have come to include complicated thought processes among the events studied. Hochberg (1954) has objected to the all-inclusive meaning of the term 'perception'.

The behavioristic position was carried to an extreme by the old behaviorist Allport (1955) in a book said to deal with theories of perception. Allport arrived at the conclusion that perception could be regarded as a discriminatory response (p. 53). We shall attempt to find out how Allport came to believe that reference to perceptual experience could be omitted. Allport illustrated his point of view by an example taken from color vision. A person unfamiliar with the color names of the English language is trained to react to some part of the wavelength range by the word blue and to another part by the word red. Then he is presented with objects differing in hue and asked to place all objects which he would designate by the word blue in one pile and all he would designate by the word red in another. If he can do this task correctly, Allport concluded that he can 'perceive' blue and red. Perception is thus defined as a discriminatory response.

In this example Allport capitalized on the fact that we, as the result of psychophysical research on color, are able to designate in advance the range of wavelength called blue and the range called red. The problem which necessarily must be raised is how did research workers find out that different ranges of wavelength could be discriminated. The answer is obvious: by reference to perceptual experience.

Hue, as any other type of perceptual experience, cannot be inferred from a set of responses and a set of antecedent conditions, but must be defined by means of a set of responses and a set of antecedent conditions. In order to extend our knowledge about perceptual processes the point of departure must necessarily be taken in our perceptual world, in perceptual experience.

To illustrate how the term 'perception' has been broadened by behavioristically oriented research workers an examination of the so-called functionalistic approach will be undertaken. In this approach the point of view is emphasized that perceptual processes are influenced by motivational states (Bruner and Krech, eds., 1949; Blake and Ramsay, eds., 1951; Allport, 1955; Solley and Murphy, 1960). The well-known investigation by Levine, Chein, and Murphy (1942) may serve as an example of the treatment of problems of perception. Two groups of subjects, one group having had their ordinary meals and the other being deprived of food for various amounts of time, are shown a number of pictures which more or less clearly may be said to represent food objects. The subjects, children, aged 10—11 years, are asked to give their associations to the pictures.

As will be seen, merely the conditions under which the responses are emitted have been specified. No experiment has been performed to define the experiences of the subjects when presented with the pictures. Thus it can merely intuitively be assumed that the experiences are perceptual in nature. Apparently the subjects in associating to the pictures may report on imaginary and thought experiences as well as on perceptual experiences.

This point is important in investigating the possible effect of motivational states on perceptual processes. A psychologist would hardly maintain that imaginary processes were not influenced by motivational states. The problem is whether what has traditionally been regarded as perceptual processes are influenced. Evidently the design of Levine, Chein, and Murphy — as is true of all the studies in this approach (cf.

Saugstad and Schioldborg, 1965; Saugstad, 1966) — wipes out the distinction between perceptual and imaginary experiences. This distinction is fundamental. Without it no science would be possible. There is ample evidence to support it.

It seems safe to state that whenever some set of perceptual experiences has been defined, the perceptual experiences are obtainable only when certain temporal relationships hold true. Thus we know that the experience of color depends upon the length of time the stimulation has lasted, and further that after cessation of stimulation the experience changes. First a so-called positive after-image and then a negative after-image are obtained. Then the experience is of some grayish appearance. These differences in experience are accompanied by biochemical and electrophysiological changes. The fact that experiences resembling those under stimulation are obtainable in the so-called eidetics and in hallucinations cannot overthrow the distinction between perceptual and imaginary processes in perceptual research. It is merely as a result of an extreme behavioristic orientation that this distinction has been overlooked.

Investigations in which the distinction between perceptual and imaginary processes is overlooked might be expected to yield deviating results. This is what is found when the various studies are carefully examined (cf. Saugstad and Schioldborg, 1965; Saugstad, 1966).

Research in perception has revealed that an exact control of temporal relationships in many instances is essential. Therefore, an ideal design for an experiment in perception is one where the response is emitted under the presence of the stimulation. This is an ideal, but instead of disregarding the problems raised by this ideal design the research worker should demonstrate his creativity in devising techniques for controlling the temporal relationships. As Smith (1957) has emphasized, psychological processes are processes over time. To achieve rigorous definitions of the various types of experiences a number of temporal constants will probably have to be determined. A psychological theory will ultimately contain a number of temporal constants determined empirically.

A reasonable requirement of a study aiming at investigating

the effect of some condition on some type of psychological processes must be that these processes have first been defined. Thus if the effect of states of motivation on perceptual processes is to be investigated, the processes expected to be affected must first be defined. A design demonstrating the effect of states of motivation on perceptual processes would have to be of the following type. First a set of perceptual experiences is rigorously defined under some specific condition of motivation by reference to some definite stimulation and a set of responses. Then it must be demonstrated that under another condition of motivation, but with the same conditions of stimulation, the set of responses is changed so as to necessitate another definition. Obviously this requirement is not easily met.

The same requirement as that stated above must also be met by investigations of the effect of some learning procedure on perceptual processes. First a set of perceptual experiences must be rigorously defined. Then some training procedure must be introduced. Finally it must be demonstrated that a new definition is required in the situation involving the original set of antecedent conditions. As a result of the apparently enormous richness of our perceptual and thought experiences a design meeting this requirement is difficult to create. Most of the studies carried out on this problem suffer from the weakness that the research worker fails to achieve a rigorous definition of the experiences involved when the subject is first presented in a situation involving the set of antecedent conditions. Solley and Murphy (1960) and their colleagues have performed a number of studies on the effect of learning on what they regard as the experience of figure-ground. They use a material representing figures drawn by lines. The figures may give the experience of some particular figure-ground, but they may also give rise to a number of other experiences. Before the training procedure is applied it must be demonstrated that the subjects have some set of perceptual experiences which may be rigorously defined by means of some set of antecedent conditions and some set of responses. This definition is not provided and no conclusion can be drawn from the studies (cf. Saugstad, 1965). The same weakness as that inherent in the studies by Solley and Murphy and their co-workers is found in the studies on perceptual learning by Gibson and Gibson (1955). Again we are ignorant about the experiences of the subjects when they are first presented with the material.

The concentration of behavioristically oriented research workers on the specification of the conditions under which the set of responses is obtained has led to an inadequate reference to the perceptual experiences and to the set of antecedent conditions. However, in its emphasis on the registration of the response the behavioristic movement has contributed to the development of a balanced view on the study of perception and of psychology in general. Schematically the history of the study of perception may be described in the following way.

The pioneer research workers in psychophysics may be said to have put a one-sided emphasis on the set of antecedent conditions, on the description of the stimulation in terms of physical energy. In a number of cases these research workers were successful in creating rigorously defined concepts. However, they tended to confuse the set of conscious experiences to be defined with the set of responses. Thus, these experiences tended to serve the double function of being concepts as well as experiences reported upon in the observations.

In the period of phenomenology, and also in the so-called introspective period of Wundtian psychology, a one-sided concentration was applied to the set of experiences, or processes, to be studied. The reference to a set of antecedent conditions and to a set of responses was neglected, the result being that this approach to psychology tended to be merely a labeling of conscious elements, or experiences.

Finally in the period of behavioristics a one-sided emphasis was placed on the set of responses, resulting in a neglect of the fact that the organism studied is a perceiving and thinking organism.

List of references

Adams, D. K. Experimental studies of adaptive behaviour in cats. *Comp. Psychol. Monogr.*, 1929, no. 27.

Allport, F. H. *Theories of perception and the concept of structure.* New York: Wiley, 1955.

Bergman, G. The contribution of John B. Watson. *Psychol. Rev.*, 1956, *63*, 265—276.

Bills, A. G. Changing views of psychology as science. *Psychol. Rev.*, 1938, *45*, 377—394.

Binet, A. *L-étude expérimentale de l'intelligence,* Paris: Schleicher Frères, 1903.

Blake, R. R. & Ramsay, G. V. (eds.). *Perception: an approach to personality.* New York: Ronald, 1951.

Boring, E. G. *A history of experimental psychology.* 2. ed., New York: Appleton-Century-Crofts, 1950.

Bridgman, P. W. [1928] *The logic of modern physics.* New York: Macmillan, 1949.

Bruner, J. S. & Krech, D. (eds.). *Perception and personality: a symposium.* Durham: Duke Univ. Press. 1950.

Brunswik, E. *Perception and the representative design of psychological experiments.* Berkely: Univ. Cal. Press, 1956.

Ebbinghaus, H. *Gründzüge der Psychologie.* I. Leipzig: Veit, 1902.

Ehrenfels, Chr. von. Ueber «Gestaltqualitäten». *Vtljschr. Wiss. Philos.*, 1890, *14*, 249—292.

Eisler, H. Magnitude scales, category scales, and Fechnerian integration. *Psychol. Rev.*, 1963, *70*, 243—253.

Ekman, G. Some aspects of psychophysical research. In W. A. Rosenblith (ed.): *Sensory communication.* M. I. T. Press and Wiley & Sons, 1961.

Estes, W. K. The statistical approach to learning theory. In S. Koch (ed.): *Psychology: a study of a science.* Vol. 2, New York: McGraw-Hill, 1959. 380—491.

Fechner, G. T. *Elemente der Psychophysik,* I, II, Leipzig: Breitkopf & Härtel, 1860.

Fieandt, K. von. *Varseblivningens psykologi.* Helsingfors: Söderström, 1956.

Frank, P. *Modern science and its philosophy.* Cambridge: Harvard Univ. Press, 1950.

From, F. *Om opplevelsen af andres adferd.* 2. opl. København: Nyt Nordisk forlag Arnold Busck, 1953.

Garner, W. R. Hake, H. W. & Eriksen, C. W.: Operationism and the concept of perception. *Psychol. Rev.*, 1956, *63*, 149—159.

Gelb, A., Die Farbenkonstanz der Sehdinge. In A. Bethe (ed.): *Handb. norm. path. Physiol.* XII, 1. Berlin: Springer, 1929. 594—678.

Gibson, J. J. *The perception of the visual world.* Boston: Houghton Mifflin, 1951.

Gibson, J. J. Perception as a function of stimulation. In S. Koch (ed.): *Psychology: a study of a science.* Vol. 1, New York: McGraw-Hill, 1959. 456—501.

Gibson, J. J. & Gibson, E. Perceptual learning: differentiation or enrichment? *Psychol. Rev.,* 1955, 62, 32—41.

Ginsberg, A. Hypothetical constructs and intervening variables *Psychol. Rev.,* 1954, *61,* 119—131.

Goude, G. On fundamental measurement in psychology. *Stockholm Studies in Psychol.,* 2. Stockholm: Almquist & Wiksell, 1962.

Graham, C. H. Visual perception. In S. S. Stevens (ed.): *Handbook of experimental psychology.* New York: Wiley, 1951. 868—920.

Graham, C. H. Sensation and perception in an objective psychology. *Psychol. Rev.,* 1958, *65,* 65—76.

Guthrie, E. R. *The psychology of learning.* New York: Harper, 1935.

Guthrie, E. R. Association by contiguity. In S. Koch (ed.): *Psychology: a study of a science.* Vol. 2. New York: McGraw-Hill, 1959. 158—195.

Guthrie, E. R. & Horton, G. P. *Cats in a puzzle box.* New York: Rinehart, 1946.

Helmholtz, H., von. [1856-66.] *Handbuch der physiologischen Optik,* I, II, III, 3. Aufl. Leipzig: Voss, 1909—1911.

Hempel, C. G. *Fundamentals of concept formation in empirical science.* Int. Encycl. Unif. Science, II, 7. Chicago: Univ. Chicago Press, 1952.

Hering, E. *Grunzüge der Lehre vom Lichtsinn.* Leipzig: Engelmann, 1905—1920.

Hilgard, E. *Theories of learning.* 2. rev. ed. New York: Appleton-Century-Crofts, 1956.

Hochberg, J. Perception: towards the recovery of a definition. *Psychol. Rev.,* 1956, 63, 400—405.

Hull, C. L. *Principles of behavior.* New York: Appleton-Century-Crofts, 1943.

Humphrey, G. *Thinking.* London: Methuen, 1951.

Husserl, E. [1913.] *Ideen zu einer reinen Phänomenologie und phänomenologischen Philosophie.* Drittes Buch. *Die Phänomenologie und die Fundamente der Wissenschaften.* Husserliana, V. Haag: Nijhoff, 1952.

Judd, D. B. Basic correlates of the visual stimulus. In S. S. Stevens (ed.): *Handbook of experimental psychology.* New York: Wiley, 1951. 811—867.

Junge, K. *Some problems of measurement in psychophysics. A. theoretical study.* (In press.) Oslo: Universitetsforlaget.

Katz, D. Der Aufbau der Farbwelt. *Z. Psychol., Ergb.* 7, 1930.

Koch, S. (ed.). *Psychology: A study of a science.* Vols. 1, 2, 3. New York: McGraw-Hill, 1959.

Koch, S. Clark L. Hull. In W. K. Estes *et al.: Modern Learning Theory.*
New York: Appleton-Century-Crofts, 1954. 1—176.

Koffka, K. *Principles of Gestalt psychology.* New York: Harcourt, Brace, &
Co., 1935.

Köhler, W. *Intelligenzprüfungen an Anthropoiden.* I. Berlin: König. Akad.
Wiss., 1917.

Köhler, W. *The place of value in a world of facts.* New York: Liveright, 1938.

Levine, R., Chein, I., & Murphy, C. The relation of intensity of a need to
the amount of perceptual distortion: a preliminary report. *J. Psychol.,*
1942, 13, 283—293.

MacCorquodale, K. & Meehl, P. E. Operational validity of intervening constructs. *Psychol. Rev.,* 1948, 55, 95—107.

Mach, E. [1886.] *Die Analyse der Empfindungen.* 4. Aufl. Jena: Fischer,
1903.

MacLeod, A. B. The place of phenomenological analysis in social psychology.
In J. H. Rohrer & M. Sherif (eds.): *Social psychology at crossroads.* New
York: Harper, 1951.

Marx, M. H. (ed.). *Psychological theory.* New York: Macmillan, 1951.

Marx, M. H. (ed.). *Theories in contemporary psychology.* New York:
Macmillan, 1963.

Merlau-Ponty, M. *Phénoménologie de la perception.* Paris: Gallimard, 1945.

Mill, J. S. [1843.] *A system of logic.* London: Longmans, Green, 1956.

Müller, J. *Handbuch der Physiologie des Menschen.* I, II. Coblentz: Hölscher,
1834—1840.

Pawlow, J. P. [1923.] Zwanzigjährige Erfahrungen mit dem objectiven
Studium der höheren Nerventätigkeit (des Verhaltens) der Tiere. *Sämt-
liche Werke.* B. IV. L. Pickenhain (ed.). Berlin: Akademie-Verlag,
1953.

Poincaré, H. [1902] *La science et l'hypothèse.* Paris: Flammarion, 1956.

Postman, L. & Tolman, E. C. Brunswik's probabilistic functionalism. In
S. Koch (ed.)· *Psychology: a study of a science.* Vol. 1. New York:
McGraw-Hill, 1959. 502—564.

Purkinje, J. *Beobachtungen und Versuche zur Physiologie der Sinne.* II.
Berlin: Reimer, 1825.

Rubin, E. *Synsoplevede figurer. Studier i psykologisk analyse.* København:
Gyldendal, 1915.

Rubin, E. Über Gestaltwahrnehmung. *VIIIth International Congress of
Psychology.* Proceedings and papers, 1927. Also in Rubin, E.: *Experi-
menta Psychologica.* Copenhagen: Munksgaard, 1949. 9—17.

Saugstad, P. Problem-solving as dependent on availability of functions.
Brit J. Psychol., 1955, 46, 191—198.

Saugstad, P. Availability of functions. A discussion of some theoretical aspects.
Acta Psychol., 1958, 13, 384—400, and *Nord. Psychol.,* 1958, 10, 216—
232.

Saugstad P. Effect of reward and punishment on the visual perception of
figure-ground. *Scand. J. Psychol.,* 1965, 6. (In Press.)

Saugstad, P. Effect of food deprivation on perception-cognition. *Psychol. Bull.,* 1966, 64. (In Press.)

Saugstad, P. & Saugstad, A. The duplicity theory an evaluation. *Advances in Ophthalmology,* 1959, 9, 1—51.

Saugstad, P. & Schioldborg, P. Value and size perception. *Scand. J. Psychol.,* 1966, 7. (In Press.)

Skinner, B. F. *The behavior of organisms.* New York: Appleton-Century-Crofts, 1938.

Skinner, B. F. A case history in scientific method. In S. Koch (ed.): *Psychology: a study of a science.* Vol. 2. New York: McGraw-Hill, 1959. 359—379.

Smith, G. Visual perception: an event over time. *Psychol. Rev.,* 1957, 64, 306—313.

Solley, C. & Murphy, G. *Development of the perceptual world.* New York: Basic Books, 1960.

Spence, K. W. The methods and postulates of 'behaviorism'. *Psychol. Rev.,* 1948, 55, 67—78. Also in M. H. Marx (ed.): *Theories in contemporary psychology.* New York: Macmillan, 1963. 272—286.

Spence, K. W. Theoretical interpretations of learning. In S. S. Stevens (ed.): *Handbook of experimental psychology.* New York: Wiley, 1951. 690—729.

Stevens, S. S. Psychology and the science of science. *Psychol. Bull.,* 1939, 36, 221—263. Also in M. H. Marx (ed.): *Theories in contemporary psychology.* New York: Macmillan, 1963. 47—76.

Stevens, S. S. (ed.). *Handbook of experimental psychology.* New York: Wiley, 1951.

Stevens, S. S. Ratio scales, partition scales and confusion scales. In H. Gulliksen & S. Messick (eds.): *Psychological scaling: theory and applications.* New York: Wiley, 1960.

Stumpf, C. Zur Einteilung der Wissenschaften. *Abh. königl. Preuss. Akad. Wiss., zu Berlin, Phil.-hist. Classe,* 1906, 1—94.

Thorndike E. L. [1898]. *Animal intelligence, experimental studies.* New York: Macmillan, 1911.

Thurstone, L. L. A law of comparative judgement. *Psychol. Rev.,* 1927, 34, 273—286.

Tichtner, E. B. *An outline of psychology.* New York: Macmillan, 1896.

Tolman, E. C. [1932]. *Purposive behavior in animals and men.* Berkeley: Univ. Calif. Press, 1949.

Tolman, E. C., Operational behaviorism and current trends in psychology. *Proc. 25th. Anniv. Celebr. Inaug. Grad. stud.* Los Angeles: Univ. South Calif. Press, 1936. Also in M. H. Marx (ed.): *Psychological Theory.* New York: Macmillan, 1954. 87—102.

Tolman, E. C. Principles of purposive behavior. In S. Koch (ed.): *Psychology: a study of a science.* New York: McGraw-Hill, 1959. 92-137.

Tranekjær Rasmussen, E. *Bevidsthedsliv og Erkendelse.* København: Munksgaard, 1956.

103

Watson, J. B. *Psychology from the standpoint of a behaviorist.* 3. rev. ed. Philadelphia: Lippincott 1929.

Wertheimer M. Untersuchungen zur Lehre von der Gestalt. II. *Psychol. Forsch.,* 1923, *4,* 301—350.

Woodworth, R. S. *Experimental psychology.* New York: Holt, 1938.

Woodworth, R. S. & Schlosberg, H. *Experimental psychology.* Rev. ed. London: Methuen, 1961.

Wright, G. H. von. *A treatise on induction and probability.* London: Routledge & Kegan Paul, 1951.

Wright, W. D. *Researches on normal and defective colour vision.* London: Kimpton, 1946.

Wundt, W. *Grundzüge der physiologischen Psychologie.* Leipzig: Engelmann, 1874.

For Product Safety Concerns and Information please contact our EU
representative GPSR@taylorandfrancis.com
Taylor & Francis Verlag GmbH, Kaufingerstraße 24, 80331 München, Germany

9 780367 857219